DEVIL'S ADVOCATES

DEVIL'S ADVOCATES

CARRIE

NEIL MITCHELL

auteur

Acknowledgments

Neil Mitchell would like to thank John Atkinson of Auteur Publishing for his support and input during the writing of this book. Thanks are also due to fellow Devil's Advocates Anne Billson, James Rose, Ian Cooper and Jez Conolly. For various reasons a doff of the cap is proffered in the direction of Alan Hodge, Glenn Ward, John Berra, Gabriel Solomons, Scott Jordan Harris and Hel Jones. My parents, family and friends have my utmost respect and undying appreciation for encouraging me during this, and other, projects.

First published in 2013 by
Auteur, 24 Hartwell Crescent, Leighton Buzzard LU7 1NP
www.auteur.co.uk
Copyright © Auteur 2013

Series design: Nikki Hamlett at Cassels Design
Set by Cassels Design www.casselsdesign.co.uk
Printed and bound by CPI Group (UK) Ltd, Croydon, CR0 4YY

British Library Cataloguing-in-Publication Data
A catalogue record for this book is available from the British Library

ISBN: 978-1-906733-72-8

Contents

INTRODUCTION

Brian De Palma's tenth feature length film, *Carrie* (1976), was adapted for the screen by Lawrence D. Cohen from Stephen King's 1974 debut novel. Produced by Paul Monash and released by United Artists, the film starred Sissy Spacek in the title role alongside Piper Laurie as her mother, Margaret White. The supporting cast featured early or debut big screen appearances by Amy Irving, Nancy Allen, William Katt, PJ Soles, Betty Buckley and John Travolta.

SYNOPSIS

Bates High School teenager Carrie White is the shy, friendless outsider among her classmates. Class rebel Chris Hargensen acts as the ringleader in making the girl the butt of their jokes. In the locker room after a gym class Carrie has her first period. Unaware of what is happening to her a terrified Carrie appeals for help but is instead mocked by the other girls, including the normally well behaved Sue Snell, who throw tampons and sanitary towels at the helpless girl. Gym teacher Miss Collins comes to Carrie's aid and admonishes the rest of the class for their rowdy, cruel behaviour. As she tries to calm Carrie down a lightbulb blows above their heads.

Further strange incidents begin to happen around Carrie at times when the put-upon teenager is under stress. Her unhappy home-life, dominated by her mother Margaret, a Christian Fundamentalist, adds to Carrie's feelings of oppression and alienation by and from those around her. Sue Snell, feeling guilty for the part she played in Carrie's cruel humiliation, conceives a plan to make it up to the troubled teenager by asking her boyfriend, Tommy Ross, on whom Carrie has a crush, to ask the girl to the prom. Having been banned from the prom by Miss Collins for acting out in the detention given to the girls for their actions, Chris, along with her delinquent boyfriend, Billy Nolan, hatches her own, malicious, plan for Carrie.

Carrie defies her mother's objections and accepts Tommy's invitation to the prom. Growing in confidence and seeking acceptance from her peers, Carrie is also becoming aware of her latent telekinetic abilities – abilities her God-fearing mother attributes to being the work of Satan. When one final appeal by Margaret White fails to dissuade her, now openly rebellious, daughter from attending the prom, the pieces of Chris' plan begin to fall into place. Chris' friends rig the voting in the prom King & Queen ballot, ensuring that Carrie and Tommy are the winners. Carrie's fairytale evening, including kissing Tommy on the dance-floor, reaches giddy new heights when the winners of the ballot are announced. Taking to the stage to be crowned Queen alongside Tommy's King, Carrie believes herself to have finally been accepted as one of the crowd. Unbeknownst to Carrie, Chris and Billy are hiding under the stage, preparing to pull a rope attached to a bucket of pigs' blood Billy placed in the rafters above the stage.

At the moment of coronation, Chris yanks the rope and the blood drenches the unsuspecting girl, the bucket knocking Tommy unconscious on its way down. With her dreams crushed by this latest public humiliation, and believing everyone to be laughing at her, Carrie snaps, unleashing her telekinetic powers with a murderous fury. Returning home, Carrie is forced by her mother into one last, bloody display of her supernatural powers.

CARRIE

When that hand comes out of the grave in Carrie *at the end. Man, I thought I was going to shit in my pants.*

Those words, spoken by Stephen King when asked about the scariest moments in the films adapted from his work in a 1986 interview with American Film magazine , is a sure fire, and telling, seal of approval from the 'Master of Horror' that Brian De Palma's *Carrie* is perhaps the finest adaptation of King's work. That King, who admired *Stand by Me* (1986, Reiner), *The Shawshank Redemption* (1994, Darabont), *The Green Mile* (1999, Darabont) and *The Mist* (2007, Darabont), but was disappointed in many of the adaptations of his work, including Stanley Kubrick's take on *The Shining* (1980), instantly referred to *Carrie* and to a sequence entirely absent from his novel speaks volumes for De Palma's success in both adapting and adding his own idiosyncratic fingerprints to King's material. The 2006 documentary, *Going to Pieces: The Rise and Fall of the Slasher Film* (McQueen), has special effects maestro Tom Savini openly admitting that the end sequence of Carrie directly inspired the coda sequence of Sean Cunningham's *Friday the 13th* (1980). That someone who has devoted his entire career to devising and delivering ever more technically impressive and visually gruesome effects and set pieces for horror movies was so struck by *Carrie's* simple yet devastating final moments is, like King's reaction to the same sequence, profoundly telling. *Carrie* not only garnered the director his first critical and box office hit, elevating him into the same league as fellow 'movie brats'[1] Francis Ford Coppola, Martin Scorsese and Steven Spielberg, but secured Academy Award nominations in the Best Actress and Best Supporting Actress categories for Sissy Spacek and Piper Laurie respectively. The adaptation also helped lodge the name of Stephen King firmly in the public's consciousness, a place it has remained ever since.

Much like the conflicted personality of its central character, *Carrie* is a film with more than one identity and stands out even within the dominant American horror films of the 1970s, a genre that Robin Wood called '*the most important of all*' (1986: 84) of that era and '*perhaps the most progressive, even in its overt nihilism*' (ibid.). Not as relentlessly oppressive or graphically violent as William Friedkin's *The Exorcist* (1973), Tobe Hooper's *The Texas Chain Saw Massacre* (1974), Wes Craven's *The Last House on the Left* (1972)

A literal reflection of Carrie's fractured psyche and one of many dual/mirrored images

and *The Hills Have Eyes* (1977) or George A. Romero's *Dawn of the Dead* (1978), and never having encountered the opprobrium of the 'moral majority', the cult worship or censorship issues that variously attached themselves to those films, *Carrie* is nonetheless every bit as bleak and critical of the social environment from which it emerged as its more notorious siblings. The visual romanticism, lyricism and moments of humour that De Palma used to counteract the movie's more horrifying moments has seen it cited in academic and critical circles as an influence on both the cycle of teen-oriented horror movies and the gross-out teen comedies that emerged in the late '70s and early '80s.

It is the indelible figure of Carrie White herself that makes the movie such an interesting candidate for the Devil's Advocates series. A profoundly sad, pathetic wretch who undergoes a classic, clichéd even, swan-like transformation, only for it to mutate her into something uncontrollable, supernaturally powerful and vengeful, Carrie White is not only the runt of her peers, but is also the awkward runt of her contemporaneous fictional monstrous counterparts. Where Leatherface (Gunnar Hansen) in *The Texas Chain Saw Massacre* is human but wholly grotesque, Jennifer (Camille Keaton) in *I Spit on Your Grave* (1978, Zarchi) a crudely drawn avenging angel and *The Omen*'s (1976, Donner) Damien (Harvey Spencer Stephens) the literal embodiment of evil, Carrie White is a richly complex character that engenders a range of contrasting emotions in the viewer. To inspire pity, lust, revulsion, fear, empathy, disassociation, maternal or paternal instincts and the memories of those real life Carrie Whites – minus the fantastical abilities but possessed of that 'otherworldly' aura – that every school has is a remarkable, and unusual, achievement. Frankenstein's Monster may evoke similar emotions but, crucially, lust and parental instincts are not among them. Carrie White was a new 'monster' for the modern world – an adolescent girl, frightening to her peers, unsettling for the adult patriarchy and confusing to herself. Her tragic journey from self discovery to self destruction may ultimately be rendered in the aesthetics of Grand Guignol theatre and the supernatural, but Carrie White is a recognisably real 'monstrous' figure. That Spacek so profoundly inhabited the skin of the character at the age of twenty six and De Palma, at the age of thirty five, instinctively knew that his vision of King's material would work points to this aspect of the narrative. We all know or remember those outcasts from school, that all consuming world where we spent our formative years, and we either witnessed, participated in or experienced firsthand the soul destroying humiliations dished out to those who didn't quite fit in.

On its release De Palma's film was not short of influential champions, with Pauline Kael calling it '*a terrifyingly lyrical thriller*' in her review for The New Yorker and Roger Greenspun in the 1977 January/February issue of Film Comment dubbing it, in relation to the previous fall's releases, '*one of the few recent achievements in American movies*'. The Washington Post film critic at the time, Gary Arnold, wrote that King's material '*provided De Palma with the opportunity to synthesize every aspect of his filmmaking talent*'. *Carrie*'s Gothic horror supernatural elements and socially timeless themes – bullying, familial breakdown, coming-of-age, high school peer pressure, female sexuality, religious repression – allied to Pino Donnagio's Herrmannesque score, Paul Hirsch's editing, Mario Tosi's cinematography and Jack Fisk's art direction combined to create a film as fully realised as any in the critically divisive film-maker's career. However, *Carrie*, like De Palma, was not universally praised, with Janet Maslin in her Newsweek review accusing the director of '*off-hand misogyny*' (a complaint that has dogged De Palma throughout his career) and the film of '*an air of studied triviality*'.[2] Similarly, Richard Eder, writing in The New York Times thought '*It is a mess, with bits of salvage floating usefully around in it*', while critic Ian Christie casually dismissed the entire exercise as being '*downright silly*'.[3]

The subsequent plethora of academic essays and critical articles, both pro and anti the film and its director, by the likes of Carol J Clover, Barbara Creed, Robin Wood and Eyal Peretz, and the movies influenced by De Palma's film (including *The Medusa Touch*

[1978, Gold], *Jennifer* [1978, Mack], *Patrick* [1978, Franklin], and De Palma's own *The Fury* [1978]) that followed in its wake, coupled with box office returns of $35 million ($135 million in today's money) from a $1.8 million budget, all helped to cement *Carrie's* status as a 'classic' – academically debated, influential and popular with the critical establishment and paying public alike. If further proof were needed of the enduring appeal of King's source material, and the difficulty in matching De Palma's onscreen vision of it, *Carrie* has been followed by: a belated sub-par sequel, *The Rage: Carrie 2* (1999, Shea), in which Amy Irving reprised her role of Sue Snell, the sole survivor of the prom night massacre; one ill-received and short lived stage musical featuring Betty Buckley as Margaret White; an unofficial stage musical parody, *Scarrie: The Musical*; and David Carson's 2002 television movie adaptation (more akin to King's novel than De Palma's movie). At the time of writing, an oft mooted and dispiritingly inevitable remake of De Palma's film by MGM and Screen Gems is in production for a 2013 release. Kimberly Pierce (*Boys Don't Cry*, 1999) is directing, and the cast includes Chloe Moretz (*Kick-Ass*, 2010, Vaughn) in the lead role and Julianne Moore as her mother Margaret.

As well as receiving standard VHS, DVD and Blu-ray releases, *Carrie* was the subject of a 25th Anniversary Edition complete with two forty minute-plus documentary features featuring De Palma and many of the original cast and crew, 'Visualizing Carrie' and 'Acting Carrie'. *Carrie* has retained its fascination as both a topic for academic study and as a pop culture icon, having been either aurally or visually referenced, according to IMDb, in over seventy films and television shows to date. Alongside numerous film festival screenings *Carrie* has been re-released theatrically in a number of countries over the years. On 4 December 2011 the Music Box Theater in Chicago hosted A Very *Carrie* Christmas, an evening similar to the increasingly popular Secret Cinema events in the UK. A Very *Carrie* Christmas included a pre-screening *Carrie* character parade contest, a post-screening Q&A with Piper Laurie and a live interactive commentary during the film. The one unfortunately prescient aspect of *Carrie*, the high school massacre perpetrated by a student, was addressed by King when he delivered the keynote speech at the Vermont Library Conference in June of 1999, shortly after the Columbine massacre. Entitled 'The Bogeyboys', and written in response to the incident, King spoke of the misery and resentment of high school life as he remembered it, and directly referenced *Carrie* in relation to it. That was further echoed in King's non-fiction *On Writing*, in which he wrote '*I never liked Carrie, that female version of Eric Harris and Dylan Klebold*' (2000: 88) before adding '*I pitied her and I pitied her classmates as well, because I had been one of them once upon a time*' (ibid.).

Carrie has evoked in me the same emotional reactions regardless of the passing of time or familiarity with the material. My appreciation of the subtexts of the movie, how De Palma achieved the end results, and my wider interests in the mechanics of film-making and narrative construction, have, naturally, evolved over time and with successive viewings. What I still get from the movie on a gut level, however, is an over-riding sense of sadness in seeing Carrie White's isolation, a feeling of helplessness watching her walk up onto that stage to have her dream so humiliatingly crushed, then anger at Carrie's peers, sorrow at their demise and finally a queasy sense of unsettling voyeurism from witnessing it all. *Carrie* is popcorn entertainment with an edge, the spectacle both exhilarating and depressing, gratifying and shameful. As the viewer looks at Carrie White, *Carrie* looks at the viewer; to enter into its world is to re-enter one that you have already lived through. Not in literal, violent experience perhaps but in symbolic, emotional essence, the dregs of which never fully leave the psychological bloodstream. Leatherface may appall, Jennifer may provoke and Damien may frighten, but Carrie White does more; she sucks you in and then spits you out. You may love her, hate her or want to protect her, but in the end Carrie White rejects us all, and everyone is to blame.

This study will draw from the differing factors mentioned, and my personal reactions to them and the movie as a whole, to explore *Carrie*'s journey from the page to the big screen, a journey that has seen it become a highly important part of its director's oeuvre and a classic of horror cinema.

FOOTNOTES

1. As explored in Biskind, P. *Easy Riders and Raging Bulls: How the Sex-Drugs and Rock 'N Roll Generation Saved Hollywood*, Simon & Schuster, 1998.
2. Sourced from Collings, R. (1986) *The Films of Stephen King*, San Bernardino, Borgo Press.
3. Ian Christie, *Daily Express*, 14 January, 1977.

PART ONE: BIRTH OF A MONSTER

Horror is visited upon the audience in familiar harbours: in the '70s, horror comes home.
(Crane, J.L. in Mendik, 2002: 167)

As with all movies that attain a lasting resonance and/or reverential status there is no
single defining attribute that led to *Carrie*'s standing as a classic, but rather a convergence
of diverse determining factors. Talent, happenstance, timing and prevailing social, cultural
and political climates and mores are all equally influential elements that affect a movie's
reception. In *Carrie*'s case, these factors gestated in the fledgling career of horror novelist
Stephen King, De Palma's ambitions (commercial and artistic), the climate of unrest in
America in the early 1970s and the wave of homegrown nihilistic horror movies that
both commented on and reflected the country's troubled psyche at the time. Along
with the 'paranoid conspiracy' thrillers and pointedly political movies of the time, such as
The Conversation (1974, Coppola), *The Parallax View* (1974, Pakula), *All the President's Men*
(1976, Pakula) and *Chinatown* (1974, Polanski), the horror movies released in America
in the '70s, including but not restricted to those mentioned in the introduction, were at
the forefront of cinematic responses to a sustained period of cultural upheaval, social
turbulence and political disenchantment. *Carrie*'s diverse themes, which would later gave
rise to its equally divergent readings, were both reflective of the continuing evolution of
the horror genre during the surrounding socio-political and cultural environment of the
era and imbued with universal traits and recurring cultural motifs that withstood the test
of time.

With its underlying narrative questioning of the contrasts, divisions and disillusionment
with or breakdown of the authority of the Church, home and state, *Carrie* is a clear
product of '70s America that resonates across continents and carries equal if not more
weight in today's world. In-depth analyses of American history, cinema and literary
horror, King's early forays into short story writing and De Palma's directing career to this
point exceed the remit of this project and require far more space than is available here.
But an encapsulation of the surrounding forces, both individual and collective, that led to
the writing and subsequent filming of *Carrie*, however, can give a clear picture of its place
within the popular culture of the era and offer an insight as to how De Palma and his
cast and crew capitalised on numerous factors to bring *Carrie* to the big screen.

Stephen King and *Carrie*

Hurry up, Steve, think of a monster.

With three as yet unpublished novels to his name, *The Long Walk*, *Rage* and *The Running Man*, Stephen King's *Carrie* was written as much out of economic necessity as it was out of artistic yearning. As Brian De Palma would later use King's material to provide him with the hit he so desired, the budding author (with his wife Tabitha's constant prompting) would, with the financial success of his first published novel secure both his family's immediate financial future and allow him to write on a full-time basis. With two young children to help provide for, King's income at the time came from a combination of payment for short stories for men's magazines and the salary from his position teaching English at Hampden Academy, Maine. Provoked by a female stranger who believed him incapable of writing about women, King began a short story about a teenage girl with telekinetic powers called Carietta White. In a well documented apocryphal moment, Tabby King rescued the crumpled up papers that her husband had tossed away after deciding that it wasn't worth pursuing. After being convinced by his wife to continue writing the story, King expanded his ideas over the next two years into what became *Carrie*. In *On Writing*, written whilst the author recovered from life threatening injuries received after being hit by a van in 1999, King reminisced about the inspiration for, and writing of, *Carrie*. The title character was a composite drawn from the memories of who King referred to as the two '*loneliest, most reviled girls in my class*' (King, 2000: 82) during the author's school days. Given the protective pseudonyms 'Sondra' and 'Dodie' (and 'Sandra' and 'Tina' in an introduction penned by the author for a 25th anniversary edition of *Carrie*), King's description of the girls' appearance, home lives and social status in the harsh environs of the classroom add an edge of grim, sad reality to his socially awkward, psychically blessed/cursed creation. Relating the time that he had been hired by Sondra's God-fearing mother to shift some furniture, King writes that '*dominating the trailer's living room was a nearly life-sized crucified Jesus*' before ruminating that:

> Sondra had grown up beneath the agonal gaze of this dying God, and doing so had undoubtedly played a part in making her what she was when I knew her, a timid and homely outcast who went scuttling through the halls of Lisbon High like a frightened mouse. (2000:83)

According to King, 'Dodie' and her younger brother 'Bill' were openly castigated and teased for wearing literally the same clothes day in, day out, year in, year out. After an unexpected swan-like transformation Dodie was subjected to even more taunting as her peers '*had no intention of letting her out of the box they'd put her in; she was punished for even trying to break free*' (ibid: 86). These starkly depressing memories, both personal to King but universally familiar in some degree to everyone, would help imbue *Carrie*'s narrative, both on the page and latterly onscreen, with that painful element of empathetic recognition that makes Carrie's eventual apocalyptic act of revenge more understandable, if no less monstrous. By opining that '*The girls didn't just laugh at Dodie; they hated her, too. Dodie was everything they were afraid of*' (ibid: 85), King touches on what would become one of the central themes, and critically debated issues, of both novel and film; the elements of recognition, fear and distrust shown by the dominant female characters towards the titular figure. In curiously contradictory versions of events, in *On Writing* and the *Carrie* anniversary edition introduction, King compounds the miserable details of the girls' lives by recounting how they were both dead by the age of 30 – Sondra/Sandra dying alone during an epileptic fit in her apartment and Dodie/Tina either by a self inflicted bullet to the abdomen or by hanging. Carrie's telekinetic ability was also inspired by a memory from King's school days, this time through his reading of an article in the now defunct Life Magazine. The article in question stated that some reported instances of poltergeist activity may have been the result of telekinesis and pointed to some evidence that young people may be prone to such powers, with early adolescent girls on the cusp of their first period especially susceptible. High school life is intrinsic to the enduring, cross-genre popularity of *Carrie*. From King's reminiscences of the 1950s and '60s, through the narrative contained in the novel and the film in the '70s, right through to the present day, readers and audiences are still drawn to the often uncomfortable memories it evokes. King compounds the narrative's unsettling nature by stating that '*Very rarely in my career have I explored more distasteful territory*' (ibid: 82).

King submitted the completed manuscript to Doubleday in January of 1973, who paid him a $2,500 advance against royalties. When the paperback rights were sold by Doubleday to New American Library for $400,000, of which King received half, *Carrie* became the now globally renowned author's career establishing break. First year sales of the hardback amounted to a relatively meagre (for a mass-market genre novel) 13,000 copies, but, aided in no small part by De Palma's adaptation, the paperback would go on to sell more than two and a half million copies.

Written in an epistolary, faux-documentary style centering around a report by 'The White Commission', later to be jettisoned for the screen version, *Carrie* continued an emerging trend, on the page and onscreen, for locating it's action in a tangible, contemporary American setting. Two contemporaneous publications, Ira Levin's *Rosemary's Baby*, published in 1967, and William Peter Blatty's *The Exorcist*, published in 1971, had similarly taken 'classic' horror themes – Devil worship and possession respectively – and placed them within the realms of modern, urban spaces. It was this relocating of horror narratives from their hitherto traditional locations – the historical 'foreign' locales of the worlds of Bram Stoker's *Dracula* and Mary Shelley's *Frankenstein* – into modern American settings that pushed the evolution of the genre forward and chimed with contemporary audiences. As Tony Magistrale put it in *Landscape of Fear: Stephen King's American Gothic*, Levin and Blatty's novels

> ...bring the terror back down to earth; indeed their work is a reminder that the darkest evils are always those found in our neighborhoods, in our children, and in ourselves rather than in some deserted place out among the stars. (Magistrale, 1988: 15)

Rosemary's Baby's New York apartment block, *The Exorcist's* comfortable family home and *Carrie's* high school setting, amongst many other everyday spaces in novels/films from the period, saw instantaneously familiar contemporary locations and institutions come under attack from ancient supernatural forces. Likewise, the shift away from 'classic' monsters – vampire, werewolf, ghost – to the everyday (in physical form at least) 'monsters' seen in the novels mentioned would herald the full blossoming of a new wave of horror that saw its big screen roots in another adaptation, Alfred Hitchcock's 1960 version of Robert Bloch's novel *Psycho* (published 1959). That *Psycho* was loosely based on the crimes of notorious American serial killer Ed Gein (latterly an inspiration for *The Texas Chain Saw Massacre*), is an indicator that a shift towards human 'monsters', however fanciful or fantastical their actions, was in evidence a full decade before King sat down to write *Carrie*, and closer to twenty years before De Palma direct his adaptation.

AMERICAN HORROR MOVIES IN THE 70S AND *CARRIE*

Since Psycho, *the Hollywood cinema has implicitly recognized horror as both American and familial.* (Wood, 1986: 87)

The social, cultural and political turbulence of the 1960s and '70s in America played a key role in leading many film-makers, both established and emerging, American and international and mainstream and independent, to produce works that as well as updating the horror genre for the modern age contained underlying commentaries on the state of the nation in that modern age. The civil rights movement, the spate of political assassinations, the riots and student shootings at Kent State University, the unpopular Vietnam War, rising crime, the disgraced Nixon administration, the Manson murders and the birth and subsequent death of the hippie dream had led the American public into an unprecedented period of social upheaval, introspection and disillusionment. Crucial to *Carrie*'s narrative, and to many of the subsequent academic and critical readings of the film, was the rise of feminism and the changing place of women in society – in the home, workplace and in the media – that transpired during the '60s and '70s, and the continuing fascination, that began with the emergence of the 'teenager' in the 1950s, for onscreen representations of adolescence. The shifting of gender relations and the resulting anxieties felt throughout the dominant patriarchal society (either consciously or unconsciously), coupled with the more prominent and troublesome generational divides than had previously been experienced would reflect and add another layer of complexity to *Carrie*'s female-centric, youth oriented narrative. For Carol J. Clover, in her seminal work, *Men, Women and Chain Saws: Gender in the Modern Horror Film*, the rise of feminism and the Women's Liberation movement gave Carrie White '*a language to her victimization and a new force to her anger that subsidizes her own act of horrific revenge*' (1992: 4). A female lead in a crossover coming-of-age/horror film, both of which have traditionally had a predominantly young, male audience demographic, threw up interesting issues regarding audience identification. *Carrie*, and the genre as a whole, had for Clover evolved to a point where '*we are truly in a Universe in which the sex of a character is no object*' (ibid: 20).

In contrast to the dominant themes as evinced by the 'Red Menace' science fiction and horror movies of the 1950s, where the threat came from outside forces and the enemies were largely inhuman 'foreign' entities, the horror movies that emerged out of the fraught landscape of 1970s America portrayed their all too human 'monsters' as being products of its own society. Further radical differences in themes, characterisations, visual imagery and narrative resolutions occurred either side of, and in many ways because of, the globally turbulent sixties. In the 1950s, Christian Nyby's *The Thing From Another World* (1951), a prime example of the period's dominant genre narratives, saw an Arctic research station come under attack from an alien being. Despite their differences the station's inhabitants, a mixture of military personnel and scientists, representative of dominant patriarchal authority figures, eventually defeat the threat to the established order from the external 'other'. By the 1970s, Wes Craven's *The Last House on the Left* depicted a brutal rape/murder revenge narrative occurring in and around the confines of a family residence and George A. Romero's *Dawn of the Dead* satirised contemporary consumer society with its tale of a zombie epidemic. Whereas in Nyby's film figures in authority play a dominant and heroic role throughout the narrative, in *The Last House on the Left* the avenging patriarch is reduced to the level of the rapist/murderers, leaving him a broken, grief stricken murderer. The movie's other figures of authority – police officers searching for the missing daughter – are portrayed as ineffectual, bumbling idiots, figures of fun at odds with the vicious, conscience-free killers. In *Dawn of the Dead*, all social structures have collapsed, leaving the survivors to fend for themselves against increasingly bleak odds within an unresolved narrative. The four central characters in *Dawn* – two members of a SWAT team, a traffic reporter and his TV newsroom assistant girlfriend – abandon their posts and all pretenses of working for the greater good. In a pointed moment underlining just how far the representation of figures in authority had changed between the 1950s and the '70s, Ken Foree's SWAT team member, Peter, asserts 'we're thieves and we're bad guys... that's exactly what we are'.

This was the era in which the anti-hero and vigilante revenge narratives came to prominence, both in the mainstream – Travis Bickle in Martin Scorsese's *Taxi Driver* (1976) – and the niche, genre market – Jennifer Hills in Meir Zachi's *I Spit on Your Grave*. Audience identification with these alienated, marginal and compromised characters – victims who become hero/heroines that commit monstrous acts – threw up uncomfortable moral, ethical and spiritual questions that are similarly addressed as part of *Carrie*'s multi-layered narrative. *Carrie*'s anti-Cinderella narrative, a twisted take on the biblical story of Samson with a central character explicitly intended, in De Palma's hands rather than in King's, to elicit both sympathy and revulsion, just like The Creature in *Frankenstein*, presented audiences – as Scorsese, Zachi and other film-makers did – with a contradictory figure; part victim, part hero/heroine and part monster. De Palma's career-long fascination with multiple personalities, voyeurism, morally corrupted anti-heroes, damaged females and the effects of violence on characters and audiences has perhaps never been so clearly envisioned and clinically executed as in the shattered psyche of Carrie White during her prom night rampage. *Carrie* would also efficiently and cruelly dismantle the nostalgic, rose tinted view of high school and teenage life as evinced by De Palma's friend George Lucas in *American Graffiti* (1973), a coming-of-age film that had scored significant box office success.

In terms of visual imagery, the more progressive, permissive attitudes of the 1960s had led to increasingly graphic onscreen nudity and violence, as witnessed in a wide range of films including the no-budget 'splatter' movies of Hershell Gordon Lewis, Romero's groundbreaking horror *Night of the Living Dead* (1968), Arthur Penn's true crime gangster movie *Bonnie & Clyde* (1967), Sam Peckinpah's brutal Western *The Wild Bunch* (1969) and the 'porno chic' of Gerald Damiato's *Deep Throat* (1972) and Artie Mitchell's *Behind the Green Door* (1972). Whilst *Carrie*'s outbursts of violence were less graphic than those of *The Last House on the Left* or *The Hills Have Eyes*, and its nudity not as explicitly or technically pornographic in nature, the iconic shower room sequence, for example – a carefully constructed, unsettling combination of nubile female flesh, menstrual blood and psychological trauma – would not have made it to the screen in such a provocative, complex and confrontational fashion in previous, more restrained and censorious, eras. De Palma's manipulation of audience expectations in the shower room sequence alone is a microcosm for much of the ground the director explored both before and after *Carrie*. De Palma's overt interests in sex, violence, psychological trauma and women – be they positively or negatively received by audiences, academics and critics – are fully encapsulated from *Carrie*'s catalytic outset.

Both Robin Wood, in the chapter 'The American Nightmare: Horror in the '70s' in his book *Hollywood: From Vietnam to Reagan* (1986), and Jonathan L. Crane, in his essay 'Come-on-a-My House: The Inescapable Legacy of Wes Craven's *The Last House on the Left*' (in Mendik, 2002), analyse the changing face of the genre in this period. Crane, although not mentioning *Carrie*, notes that '*in most films from this era no empowered authority figure or potent institution shields the victim from the blade of the omnipotent butcher*' (ibid: 168), while for Wood, specifically in relation to *The Texas Chain Saw Massacre* but indicative of the genre as a whole during the period, there was '*the sense of a civilization condemning itself, through its popular culture, to ultimate disintegration*' (1986: 94). Within twenty years film-makers working in the science fiction/horror genres had shifted from either surreptitiously or pointedly addressing fears of 'the other' putting the American way of life in danger to questioning that very way of life itself; it's aims, the anxieties it's actions wrought, the social inequalities entrenched within it and the institutions that upheld its values. Though not by any means confined to these genres (one need only look at how that most American of genres, the road movie, ended the 1960s and entered the '70s with the increasingly nihilistic outlooks of *Easy Rider* [1969, Hopper], *Vanishing Point* [1971, Sarafian] and *Two Lane Blacktop* [1971, Hellman]), it is in the horror movies of the era that (perhaps understandably given the nature of the genre) the most savage reflections of the country's damaged psyche were to be found. Whether the films took 'classic' horror themes and transplanted them into contemporary times (*Carrie, The Omen, It's Alive* [1974, Cohen]), or drew their narrative horrors from distinctly human crimes (*The Texas Chain Saw Massacre, The Hills Have Eyes, Halloween* [1978, Carpenter]), the genre was epitomised as a whole by visions of dysfunctional families, social breakdown, failing institutions and nihilistic resolutions. Using apt terminology Wood asserts that

in its Apocalyptic phase, the horror film, even when it is not concerned literally with the end of the world (*The Omen*), brings its own world to cataclysm, refusing any hope of positive resolution. (ibid: 154)

While conforming to many of these traits, *Carrie* also markedly differed in certain crucial areas. The dysfunctional family, social breakdown/failing institutions and nihilistic resolution are very much in evidence as prominent factors in the narrative. However, in contrast to Crane's assertion that '*the hallmark of the '70s horror film is sustained, unavoidable anguish with no promise of catharsis*' (in Mendik, 2002: 166), evident in the drawn out suffering endured by Sally in *The Texas Chain Saw Massacre*, or by the family relentlessly preyed upon in *The Hills Have Eyes*, *Carrie* was rigidly constructed with a rhythmical ebb and flow to its tension and violence, shot through with naturalism, comedy and romance. Despite United Artists' initial worries that they had a failure on their hands, De Palma's *Carrie* would benefit from the apparent aura of respectability that a literary source afforded, in similar fashion to Roman Polanski's adaptation of *Rosemary's Baby* and William Friedkin's take on *The Exorcist*. Mainstream acceptance, as highlighted by Spacek and Piper's Oscar nominations, would prove the cross-generational and cross-genre appeal of De Palma's interpretation of King's material – a teen-oriented Gothic horror narrative – something that, at the time, would never have been achieved by *The Last House on the Left*, *The Texas Chain Saw Massacre* or *I Spit on Your Grave*.

BRIAN DE PALMA AND CARRIE

I had to beg for the job. (De Palma in Knapp, 1984: 87)

Brian De Palma's onscreen fascination for psychologically tormented split personalities is a reflection of the offscreen tensions that have been an ever present divisive element in the director's now forty year-plus career. This well educated, softly spoken figure with a penchant for onscreen violence, psychological cruelty and trauma has fought a long, hard battle, sometimes wildly successfully, sometimes disastrously not, to marry the opposing forces of artistic freedom and commercial success. De Palma's first experience of directing for a major Hollywood studio, *Get to Know Your Rabbit* (1972) for Warner Bros., had been a bruising, humiliating experience. The independently minded New Yorker clashed over the tone of the film with the star, Tom Smothers, one half, along with his younger sibling, Dick, of the musical comedy team The Smothers Brothers. Despite the sizable backing of co-star Orson Welles, De Palma was eventually fired from the project and many of his scenes were either re-shot or cut from the eventual film altogether. De Palma returned to New York and independent film-making but, crucially, moved away from the French New Wave-influenced movies that had paradoxically first attracted the attentions of Hollywood and into the commercially safer territory of genre film-making. In *The Devil's Candy: The Bonfire of the Vanities Goes to Hollywood*, author Julie Salamon reflected on De Palma's problem thus:

The filmmaker was governed by conflicting impulses. He wanted to be recognized as an artist by the critical establishment, and he wanted to achieve box office success. Yet his most personal films could never have the mass appeal of more conventional movies. (1991: 28)

De Palma's own thoughts on his often contrary relationship to art, commerce and critical acceptance were encapsulated in an interview he gave to Lynn Hirschberg for Esquire in 1984, while, tellingly, sitting in Steven Spielberg's Los Angeles office. It forms part of Laurence F. Knapp's edited collection *Brian De Palma: Interviews*:

If you just want to be famous, it's better to go out and shoot somebody. This takes a lot of work. Killing someone is easy, and instantly you're famous. I want to be infamous. I want to be controversial. It's much more colorful. (2003: 90)

Passionate, talented and ambitious, De Palma was also spurred on to make his presence felt by the critical and/or commercial successes of his friends and fellow 'movie brat' directors. Spielberg's *Jaws* (1975), Martin Scorsese's *Mean Streets* (1973) and *Taxi Driver* and Francis Ford Coppola's *The Godfather* (1972) and *The Conversation* had all garnered more admiration, both critically and commercially than De Palma's contemporaneous efforts. The contrasting fates of *Sisters* (1973), a disturbing, graphic horror thriller, *Phantom of the Paradise* (1974), a fantasy horror musical reworking of *The Phantom of the Opera*, and *Obsession* (1976), a Hitchcockian psychological mystery complete with a score written by Bernard Herrmann, exemplified De Palma's frustrations. Both *Sisters* and *Phantom of the Paradise* developed a cult following and some critical championing but did not perform as well as hoped at the box office. *Obsession*, having been shelved for a year by Columbia Pictures, who had demanded changes to the film, was finally released a few months before *Carrie* in 1976. Sometimes wrongly assumed to be both a critical and commercial flop, *Obsession* was in fact a reasonably successful commercial venture, taking $4,000,000 from a $1,800,000 budget. But it also, dishearteningly for De Palma, drew a decidedly mixed critical reaction. Whereas the National Board of Review voted it into their top ten films of 1976, Pauline Kael, one of De Palma's staunchest and most influential supporters, wrote that it was *'no more than an exercise in style, with the camera whirling around nothingness'*.[1] With Hitchcock himself reportedly furious with De Palma for directing what he saw as nothing more than an updated version of *Vertigo*

(1958) (the film having grown out of a conversation between De Palma and *Obsession*'s screenwriter Paul Schrader regarding Hitchcock's classic), De Palma had once again infuriated as much as he had thrilled. Try as he might, De Palma had by 1976, and after nine previous attempts, yet to direct a movie that combined artistic credibility with box office success and cement his status in Hollywood, thereby enabling him to pursue his creative ambitions on a grander scale than he was hitherto able.

Alongside the offscreen ambitions that drove De Palma, his onscreen visions, whether they be made manifest in comedies, thrillers, musicals or horrors, showed a clear predilection for and exploration of recurring narrative themes, character traits and visual techniques . The director's genre hopping approach to film-making also betrayed a restless imaginative streak, a masterful ability to weave those recurring themes, traits and tropes between genres and an overarching fascination for visual grammar, the language of the form itself. Whatever one may think about the individual merits of the films themselves, the apparent misogyny the director is often accused of, or the perceived superficiality of his characters and plots, De Palma is clearly a technically gifted director with a deep understanding of creating tension, suspense, horror and mystery in a narrative along with instilling sympathy, empathy, revulsion or pity for characters, however sketchily drawn they may be. One need only watch the split screen bomb planting sequence in *Phantom of the Paradise* (inspired by the opening sequence of *Touch of Evil* [1958, Welles]), *Carrie*'s wordless, slow motion bucket of pigs' blood scene, the grandiose climax to *Raising Cain* (1992), which plays out over three different levels of a hotel, or the bravura twelve minute tracking shot that opens *Snake Eyes* (1998), to appreciate that De Palma is a film-maker par excellence. In *Becoming Visionary: Brian De Palma's Cinematic Education of the Senses*, Eyal Peretz would go as far as to assert that:

> De Palma is, in my opinion, the greatest contemporary investigator, at least in American cinema, of the nature and the logic of the cinematic image and should be viewed as the equal, and heir, to such great thinkers of the cinematic image as Friedrich Wilhelm Murnau, Sergei Eisenstein, Carl Theodor Dreyer, Orson Welles, Alfred Hitchcock, Vincente Minnelli, Robert Bresson, Stanley Kubrick, Pier Paolo Pasolini, and Jean-Luc Godard. (2008: 18)

Ascending/descending 'God's eye' shots are repeated throughout the movie

From the outset of his career in the '60s, De Palma experimented with a number of stylistic techniques that would be fully developed and assimilated into the recognisable auteurist style with which he is now associated.[2] De Palma's first feature length effort, *The Wedding Party*, shot between 1964 and 1966 but not released until 1969, contained many of those stylistic tropes – slow/fast motion scenes, split screen sequences and long takes and tracking shots. The French New Wave-inspired episodic, subversive comedy, *Greetings* (1968), which won a Silver Bear at the Berlin Film Festival, and its 1969 sequel *Hi, Mom!*, which along with the little seen *Murder à la Mod* (1968) reflected De Palma's intention to become the 'American Godard', via the performance documentary, *Dionysus in 69* (1970) through to the '70s movies that preceded *Carrie*, all displayed several if not all of the stylistic proclivities that would recur throughout De Palma's long career. The eighty minute *Murder à la Mod* was an exercise in experimenting with style, with the murder of a young woman replayed three times in a similar fashion to Akira Kurosawa's *Rashomon* (1958). Instead of witnessing the events from different perspectives, however, De Palma's variation on the theme was to shoot the murder in three different styles, the first being that of a TV soap, the second being a Hitchcockian suspense thriller and the final sequence as a silent movie. From *Greetings* and *Hi, Mom!* onwards De Palma would use point-of-view (POV) shots, as well as symbolic colour schemes, regularly and *Dionysus in 69* was presented entirely in split screen. The use of split screen throughout the film was inspired by a performance De Palma saw of the titular 'environmental theatre' piece, a modern take on Euripedes' *The Bacchae*, during which a fight broke out in the stalls between members of the cast and audience. With one half of the screen showing the performance and the other half showing the audience's reaction to it, *Dionysus in '69* would later be recalled in the split screen visualisation of the prom night massacre in *Carrie*. De Palma's use of split screen would gradually evolve to encompass the employment of split dioptre lenses, utilised on numerous occasions in *Carrie*, which created two planes of focus and the appearance of a fuller, deeper three dimensional space in the frame by giving equal weight to foreground and background image. 360 degree camera pans, which art director, Jack Fisk, referred to as '*show-offy*',[3] 'God's eye' shots, ascending and descending crane shots and dream/nightmare/hallucinatory sequences would all become part of De Palma's virtuoso armory.

Intertextuality, via the referencing of both his own and other directors' films, would play a significant role in this most cine-literate of film-makers career. The most overtly referenced director in De Palma films is, of course, Alfred Hitchcock, but Michelangelo Antonioni (in *Blow Out* [1981]), Orson Welles (in *Carrie*) and Jean-Luc Godard (in *Greetings* and *Hi, Mom!*) have all been invoked, either aurally or visually, in a number of his films. The Hitchcock link has been a stick which many of De Palma's detractors have used to beat him with over the years. From his first directly Hitchcock inspired effort, *Sisters*, which lifted the witnessing of a murder scenario from *Rear Window*, via the *Vertigo* inspired *Obsession*, the renaming of the school in *Carrie* as Bates High School (a nod to Anthony Perkins' killer in *Psycho*), through to *Dressed to Kill* (1980), *Body Double* (1984) and *Raising Cain*, the 'Master of Suspense' has been a point of reference for De Palma. But rather than see De Palma's co-opting of techniques and narrative themes as detrimental to the view of his oeuvre, this author subscribes to the position taken by Wood that '*the relationship of De Palma to Hitchcock is centered on a complex dialectic of affinity and difference*' (Wood, 1986: 140). De Palma views Hitchcock and his oeuvre as the epitome of film-making, both stylistically and thematically. For a director whose films clearly exhibit visual and aural repetitions, doubles (of sequences and personalities) and an overt dialogue with the art of film-making itself, it's no surprise that a director with such a bravura repertoire would (at least attempt to) pick up the baton passed on by Hitchcock and add his own distinct mark to it. Wood succinctly makes a point that even De Palma's detractors would be hard pushed to deny by stating that '*De Palma's variations on Hitchcock – confused, unsatisfactory, maddening perhaps – are never inert*' (ibid: 141). Wood is not the only critic to have given De Palma credit for this aspect of his work. In relation to Sisters being 'the first of De Palma's obsessive hommages to Alfred Hitchcock', Kim Newman writes that 'it is also the most distinctive, original and satisfying, as secure in its assimilation of Hitchcock's ideas into the director's own vision as the best of Claude Chabrol' (Newman, 1988: 121). Sometimes used as Brechtian distancing devices, sometimes employed to reflect the psyche of his characters, but always used to explore the visual grammar of storytelling on film, De Palma's rich stylistic proclivities would all play an integral role in visualising King's Carrie for the big screen.

In terms of themes, Carrie would expand upon De Palma's interest in depicting split personalities, multiple identities, duplicity, damaged psyches and emotionally conflicted personae. Issues surrounding voyeurism, sexism and violence would also form part of De Palma's recurring thematic concerns. In the films leading up to Carrie, a variety of characters exhibited one or more of these traits. Robert De Niro's Jon Rubin, who appears as one of the three lead characters in Greetings and is the central figure of its sequel, Hi, Mom!, attempts to avoid being drafted into the US Army and sent to Vietnam by espousing extreme right wing views at odds with his left leaning lifestyle. A complex figure, both comedic and unsettling, Rubin is also a Peeping Tom, a secretive peccadillo if ever there was one, an affliction he attempts to assimilate into his abortive efforts to shoot an art installation in Greetings and then a movie in Hi, Mom! Margot Kidder's character(s) in Sisters is a graduation into deeper, more disturbing territory for a De Palma character. Playing both Danielle Breton and her dead twin sister Dominique Blanchion, the psychologically scarred Danielle's murderous alter-ego, Kidder flicks between sweet natured/psychotic, flirtatious/predatory, passive/aggressive and innocent/guilty. The most flamboyantly rendered divided persona is William Finley's Winslow Leach/ The Phantom in Phantom of the Paradise. An aspiring composer, Winslow Leach is ripped off by another unscrupulous composer, Swan (Paul Williams) and then facially disfigured in a record press. Re-inventing himself as The Phantom, replete with mask and cape, Winslow/The Phantom sells his soul à la Faust to Swan, himself in the grip of a Faustian pact with Satan. Winslow/The Phantom is a typically De Palmian creation: good/bad, passive/aggressive, inconspicuous/unmistakable and peaceful and vengeful, all traits that Carrie White exhibits. In Obsession, visual duality and emotional identity play a central role in the film's Vertigo-like narrative. Sixteen years after his wife and young daughter were supposedly killed in a failed kidnap rescue attempt, businessman Michael Courtland (Cliff Robertson) meets and falls in love with Sandra Portinari (Genevieve Bujold), a dead ringer for his wife, Elizabeth, also played by Bujold. As *Obsession's* tale of guilt, redemption, memory and betrayal unfolds, all with an uncomfortable incestuous bent, Sandra is the focus of Courtland's unrelenting eye – familiar yet strange, comforting yet unsettling, loyal yet duplicitous and, most disturbingly, tangible yet taboo.

Sin, voyeurism, guilt, lust, religion, vengeance, duplicity, callousness, mental instability, cruelty, violence, sexuality, sex and sexism course through De Palma's films, both pre- and post-*Carrie*, but it is in *Carrie* that the widest expansion and assimilation of all of his styles, themes and character traits is to be found. Doubles, opposing forces, internal and external schisms, visual repetitions, aural couplings and dichotomous actions are portrayed in slow and fast motion, from high and low angles, in 360 degree camera movements, from subjective and objective viewpoints and with references to other cinematic works, in a film that as a whole contained De Palma's first real display of emotional investment in his lead character. Where King portrayed an unsympathetic central character, De Palma, through his manipulation of audience expectations and emotions, imparted the figure of Carrie White with a level of complexity that would make the character and the film as a whole far more resonant than the sum of its narratively simple parts would at first suggest. An extra layer of complexity was added via the director's views on the horror genre. In De Palma's eyes at the very least, *Carrie*, along with *Sisters* and *Phantom of the Paradise*, in many ways transcended the bounds of genre conventions. In an interview given to Cinefantastique in 1977, De Palma, when asked whether he wanted to remain in the horror genre stated:

> They never seem like horror films to me! 'Horror films' are 'Hammer Films', vampires and Frankenstein. I love those pictures, but I don't feel it's exactly what I'm doing. Maybe I'm trying to hammer out a new genre, somehow...[4]

FOOTNOTES

1. From 'The Curse' in *The New Yorker*, 22 November, 1976.
2. A handy primer for the director's work is Ashbrook, J. *The Pocket Essential: Brian De Palma*, Pocket Essentials, 2000.

3. From the 'Visualizing *Carrie*' documentary extra feature on the 25th anniversary DVD release.

4. Childs and Jones, Cinefantastique, Summer 1977.

PART 2: FROM PAGE TO SCREEN:
BRINGING *CARRIE* TO LIFE

Carrie *was worked out like a musical score.*[1]

Edgar Wright, the director of *Shaun of the Dead* (2004) and *Hot Fuzz* (2007), chose
Carrie as one of his top ten greatest films of all time in Sight & Sound magazine's 2012
poll. His comments on the movie give further credence to the above quote from De
Palma, highlighting as they do the movie's rhythmical flow and mix of contemporary and
historic cultural forms. Wright states that:

> Brian De Palma takes Stephen King's horror of adolescence and turns it into a full-
> blown and full blooded teenage pop opera. They didn't need to turn it into a musical
> – it already was one.[2]

Carrie's transition from page to screen would, however, involve numerous changes to
the style and tone of King's novel decided upon for creative and budgetary reasons by
De Palma and screenwriter Lawrence D. Cohen. Alterations to the final shooting script
(the second draft of the adaptation) were brought about by a combination of time
constraints, on set improvisation and decisions made during post-production editing.
Though the studio approved the second draft, a fairly rare occurrence in Hollywood,
United Artists would waver on the project in other areas. Under the United Artists
banner De Palma was handed a budget of $1.6 million (eventually rising to $1.8
million) within which to work, a relatively small figure even then that reflected the
uneasy relationship between the director and the studio's money men. Even given
the horror genre's commercial and critical successes during the period, United Artists
were, perhaps understandably, unconvinced that the adaptation of a debut novel by an
experienced director still looking for a major commercial success was worth risking any
more than the figure allocated. Indeed, even after post-production was completed, so
unsure were they of what they had on their hands that in the run up to the movie's first
screenings they were toying with releasing it as part of a B-movie double bill and retitled
Pray For Carrie.

It's telling that the only real problem De Palma had with the project was in relation
to those controlling the marketing of the movie. For De Palma, *Carrie* was a serious

movie, with serious points to make about the cruelty of teenagers, the insidious effects of religious fervour and the state of contemporary American society, regardless of it being wrapped up in supernatural trappings. The director was hoping to emulate the critical and commercial appeal of Polanski's *Rosemary's Baby* and Friedkin's *The Exorcist*. United Artists, however, marketed *Carrie* as cheap popcorn entertainment, with its initial screening taking place as the unbilled second part of a double bill on Halloween night 1976.

De Palma, however, has fond memories of the project as a whole, noting that he can't remember ever having so much time to conceptually visualise a movie beforehand and to being sure that '*we got the best group of actors that were around at the time*'[3] as his cast. The pre-production time De Palma had while waiting for the budget to be rubber-stamped is perhaps key to *Carrie*'s successful transition to the big screen. Able to think about the project almost at leisure, De Palma would have every conceivable visual aspect of the film worked out and story-boarded before anyone arrived on set and approached the shooting in a relaxed and confident mood, stating that '*I knew it had an incredibly sophisticated visual design*'.[4] With only minimal changes made to Cohen's second draft of the script, principle photography was completed in fifty days, with post-production work taking several more months to complete. The lengthy editing process that *Carrie* underwent is put into perspective with the knowledge that it took six weeks for editor Paul Hirsch and De Palma to construct the prom massacre alone, assembling what would become the much vaunted sequence from over 150 individual shots.

CHANGING *CARRIE*: FINAL GIRLS AND FLASHBACKS

Cohen's initial screenplay adaptation of King's novel was largely faithful to the source material, retaining the flashback structure as seen largely through the eyes of Sue Snell. Indeed, the event that opens the novel, in which a young Carrie White is reprimanded by her mother for chatting to their sunbathing, bikini-clad neighbour before a shower of stones rains down on the White household, would be retained right up to the editing process. This opening sequence was eventually ditched when a conveyor belt carrying stones to be used to destroy the White household during shooting of the film's climax jammed. All that remained of the planned mirror image opening and climactic sequences were a few brief shots of stones crashing through the ceiling, with the interior shots of the crumbling house already having been shot.

De Palma suggested numerous changes that Cohen integrated into the second draft. The high school gym teacher of the novel, Miss Desjardin, became Miss Collins, a more influential character onscreen than on paper. With Betty Buckley, who had auditioned unsuccessfully for *Phantom of the Paradise*, already in De Palma's sights for the role, the character was fleshed out to more overtly symbolise the 'good', but equally problematic, mirror image of Margaret White's 'bad' mother figure. The concept of 'good' and 'bad' in *Carrie* (and many other De Palma films) is a flexible, ambiguous one the director appears to actively enjoy undermining and complicating. As if to underline this point, and the unforgiving nature of the director's vision, in relation to *Carrie* at least, when deciding who should be killed off and who should survive the prom night massacre while listening to the pleas and cases of the cast members as to why their character's should live, De Palma would casually state '*they're all guilty, and they've all got to go*'.[5]

The two major alterations to the novel were the shifting of the focus from Sue Snell to Carrie White, and to the character of Carrie herself. Putting the teenage telekinetic at the centre of the film would demand a greater level of intimate engagement with her, and contribute to the complex dynamic of affinity and rejection De Palma hoped audiences would experience.

Whereas King's view of Carrie was largely unsympathetic and his vision of her was as '*a frog amongst swans… a chunky girl, with pimples on her neck, back and buttocks, her wet hair completely without colour*' (King, 1974: 4), De Palma had in mind a girl capable of inspiring lust and revulsion in equal measure. Intuitively deciding that an audience would be more likely to accept, and therefore emotionally invest in a more attractive (if unconventionally so) but troubled girl rather than the less appealing figure of King's novel, would be validated by Spacek's performance and the film's box office returns.

The flashback structure of the novel was transferred to the script, after The White Commission had been ditched, in the form of multiple returns to the catalytic shower room sequence. Ultimately scrapped in the editing room, with up to twenty shots removed to eliminate this structure, the film would eventually fully abandon King's format and adopt a linear structure where forward narrative momentum, and rising tension, is key to the impact of Carrie's acts. For budgetary and narrative reasons, the widespread destruction Carrie wreaks on the town of Chamberlain, renamed by De Palma along with Ewen High School to Bates, was reduced in the film to just the destruction of the school and the White household. Electing not to spend a large proportion of the budget on destroying multiple locations enabled De Palma and Cohen to reduce Carrie's world to that of school and home, thereby tightening the narrative focus and heightening the provocative dismantling of both that ran as a pointed, wider thematic undercurrent to Carrie's personal story. Rejecting the novel's death of Margaret White by heart attack (brought about by Carrie placing her hand on her mother's chest) as offering nothing of visual interest, De Palma and Cohen conceived a more fittingly dramatic and symbolic end for Carrie's mother. Strengthening the religious themes, that play such a crucial role in Carrie's alienation from those around her, Margaret would die pinned to a door-frame by kitchen utensils, flung through the air by the force of Carrie's will. Mimicking the pose of the statue of St Sebastian that Carrie is forced to pray before, Margaret White's death in De Palma hands attains a level of irony, satire and graphic impact that far outstrips her demise in the novel.

The most far reaching difference between novel and film came in the form of the film's coda sequence. The hand from the grave scene would radically shift the focus of the film from Carrie to Sue Snell, thereby throwing the audience off guard both in terms of the shock element and in terms of identification. The then emerging concept of 'the final girl' – who Clover describes as '*the one who encounters the mutilated bodies of her friends and perceives the full extent of the preceding horror and of her own peril*' (1992: 35) – is in part conformed to but complicated by the figure of Sue Snell in *Carrie*. Even as the 'good' mirror image of Chris' 'bad' girl figure, Sue Snell is marked by Carrie as 'guilty' in the 'world within the world' of her nightmare. De Palma's decision to play with the audience not only complicates the specific narrative to that point, it had a deep impact on the future of horror films as a whole.

As opposed to the 'final girl' in many horror films, Sue Snell isn't left to confront and defeat or escape from the 'evil' in *Carrie*; rather she is left traumatised and guilt-ridden, the sole surviving witness to events she, however accidentally, helped set in motion. In terms of the evolution of the genre, De Palma's use of the coda sequence firmly

The sequence that would go on to be endlessly imitated in subsequent horror movies

established 'the final scream' as a *de rigueur* aspect of the contemporary horror movie. Where horror movies of previous eras would, largely, end with the evil/monster defeated and order to the world envisioned restored, *Carrie* would finish with one final shock. Closure would be denied to both Sue Snell and the audience, and De Palma would at the very least succeed in changing the genre if not in hammering out a new one. As Jason Zinoman succinctly recounts in *Shock Value: How a Few Eccentric Outsiders Gave us Nightmares, Conquered Hollywood, and Invented Modern Horror:* "'After *Carrie,*'" Wes Craven says, "*everyone had to have a second ending*'" (2012: 168).

CARRIE'S CAST

Unusually, casting for *Carrie* took place in tandem with that for George Lucas' *Star Wars* (1977), with both directors seeing hopefuls in dual audition sessions. The cast lists of both films could have been very different, with Carrie Fisher and Melanie Griffith both reading for the lead role in De Palma's film and Amy Irving earmarked by Lucas for the role of Princess Leia in his. Spacek, the wife of art director Jack Fisk and a set decorator on *Phantom of the Paradise*, was far from De Palma's first choice for Carrie White. The director had a specific actress in mind for the role, allegedly Pamela Sue Martin, though he has never confirmed it. Spacek, still relatively inexperienced despite her assured performance alongside Martin Sheen in Terence Malick's *Badlands* (1973), was discouraged from reading for the lead role by De Palma, the director wanting her instead for the role of Carrie's nemesis, Chris Hargensen. But in keeping with the spirit of openness to suggestions and ideas that seems to have prevailed throughout the project, De Palma relented when Spacek turned up and read for the lead role dressed in dowdy clothes and with her hair smeared with Vaseline. With Irving secured to play 'good' girl Sue Snell, De Palma would replicate his casting of real life mother and daughter Mary Davenport and Jennifer Salt in *Sisters* by casting Irving's mother, Priscilla Pointer, to play Eleanor Snell. This decision was based on De Palma liking the genuine dynamic between Davenport and Salt, something that Irving not only shared with Pointer, but also with William Katt, cast as the all American apple of Carrie's eye, Tommy Ross. Irving and Katt had previously dated, and while the relationship was brief, an easy connection and genuine affection flowed between the two, giving their onscreen relationship the spark and ring of truth it required.

P.J. Soles, who would go on to attain cult status as a 'scream queen' for her roles in numerous horror movies including *Halloween*, auditioned in the red baseball cap she wears throughout the film in her role as one of Chris Hargensen's closest allies. The casting of Nancy Allen as Hargensen, the final role secured on the last day of auditions, would not only give the film its mean-spirited queen bee, it would also eventually lead to the marriage (and later divorce) of De Palma and Allen. De Palma cast John Travolta as Billy Nolan, the 'bad' guy opposite of 'good' guy Tommy Ross. Travolta was an emerging talent at the time, familiar to television viewers as part of the cast of *Welcome Back Kotter*, and to theatre-goers for roles in the musicals *Grease* and *Over There*. With *Kotter* between seasons, De Palma and Monash acted quickly to get the rising star on board. Travolta is one of a number of actors that De Palma has cast in important, career altering roles, with Robert De Niro, Kevin Costner, Michelle Pfeiffer and Melanie Griffith foremost among them. The onscreen dynamic and offscreen working relationship between Allen and Travolta impressed De Palma to the extent that he later cast them opposite each other in the Antonioni inspired *Blow Out*. As with Betty Buckley, Piper Laurie didn't audition, with De Palma, initially at the behest of an admiring United Artists executive, first sending her the script and then meeting with her in person. Having retired from acting after winning an Academy Award for her performance in Robert Rossen's *The Hustler* (1961), Laurie had made a tentative return to the profession in a television movie for PBS called *The Woman Rebel* (1976, Gladstone). In much the same

way that the role of Tony Montana in De Palma's *Scarface* (1983) would re-invigorate Al
Pacino's career in the early '80s, the role of Margaret White, and the resulting Academy
Award nomination, convinced Laurie to return to acting on a full time basis.

The blend of fresh faced newcomers, theatrical experience, award-winning know-how,
emerging talent and familial bonds created a powerful dynamic which De Palma would
exploit fully onscreen. Pitting the upcoming Spacek against the established Laurie,
placing Irving together with Pointer and Katt, the ebullient Allen with the wisecracking
Travolta and putting the similarly aged, but more experienced, Buckley in charge of the
girls instilled the required levels of tension, competitiveness, attraction, humour and
understanding necessary between cast members for their characters to come to life
onscreen. During the week-long rehearsals prior to shooting commencing, De Palma
would have the classmates engage in a variety of high school acts, including the voting
of class reps. To further strengthen Carrie's palpable feelings of isolation and alienation
onscreen, De Palma, having called Spacek into a room where they were assembled, had
the cast members playing her classmates tease and shun her. A familiar ploy used by
many film-makers, this off-screen manipulation of emotions would also be deployed by
De Palma during shooting. Sue Snell's distressed look during the sequence in which Miss
Collins berates the girls and hands out the detention is genuinely pained. Buckley, the
figure of authority onscreen who had become friendly with Irving off-screen, was placed
behind the camera by De Palma during Irving's close up shots and asked to hurl a litany
of abuse at the young actress. Similarly, Chris' pained, flustered and angry reaction to
being slapped by Miss Collins during the following detention session was down to De
Palma's insistence that Buckley slap Allen for real. The scene was repeatedly re-shot until
the director was happy that Allen's reaction had a suitably genuine emotion behind it.

Having experimented with improv sessions during rehearsals, where the dynamics
between the whole cast and between individuals was realised from the potential De
Palma had gambled on, the director allowed a certain amount of liberation, in terms of
dialogue and actions, during filming. Laurie fought to keep the line '*red, I knew it would
be red*' in relation to Carrie's prom dress, even though the dress had changed from
the scripted red to a pink outfit, arguing that in Margaret's eyes the dress *was* red. The
actress also argued the case for her post-massacre monologue to remain, when De
Palma toyed with cutting it, and brought her own interpretation to Margaret's demise,

adding in the clearly sexualised moans and groans that gave her death throes an added level of eroticised, beatific anguish that would complement the mise-en-scène. De Palma would instigate spontaneity into the filming, if not the fully envisioned framework, by asking Buckley to dispense with the scripted dialogue for her talk with Carrie at the prom and extemporise something drawn from memories of her own actual prom night. The flexibility afforded to the cast within a rigidly structured visual scheme contributed to the dual forces of artifice and verisimilitude noticeable throughout the film.

CARRIE'S CREW

De Palma's principal crew consisted of returning and future collaborators and talented individuals who would go on to forge successful careers in their chosen fields. A small number of the crew (and cast) would continue to be associated with King's novel and De Palma's film via their involvement with *The Rage: Carrie II*, the 2002 TV movie and the ill-fated stage musical. *Carrie*'s producer, Paul Monash, who amassed a sizable body of writing credits, included the screenplays for *Salem's Lot* (1979, Hooper) and *The Friends of Eddy Coyle* (1973, Yates), would go on to produce the lacklustre sequel and act as consulting producer on the David Carson directed TV movie. Associate producer, Louis A. Stroller, a largely minor figure in *Carrie*'s off-screen story, would later work with De Palma as an executive producer on both *Scarface* and *Snake Eyes*. Italian-American cinematographer Mario Tosi would only collaborate with De Palma on *Carrie*, which – along with the Emmy nomination he received for his work on the 1976 TV drama *Sybil* (Petrie) – remains the artistic highlight of his career. Tosi was brought on board after De Palma and the original DOP, Isidore Mankofsky, clashed during the early stages of the production, and Mankofsky departed.

Editor Paul Hirsch, whose other credits include *Star Wars*, for which he shared the Academy Award for Best Film Editing with Marcia Lucas and Richard Chew, *Ray* (2004, Hackford) for which he was nominated in the same category, and *Source Code* (2011, Jones), has been a regular part of De Palma's projects from his earliest days onwards. Working in conjunction with the hands-on De Palma, Hirsch also edited *Hi, Mom!*, *Sisters*, *Phantom of the Paradise*, *Obsession*, *The Fury*, *Blow Out*, *Raising Cain*, *Mission: Impossible* (1996) and *Mission to Mars* (2000) for his longtime friend and associate. Spacek's husband, Jack Fisk, the production designer on the visually flamboyant *Phantom of the Paradise* would act as art director on *Carrie*, with set decoration handled by Robert Gould, now the veteran in that area of fifty five films and counting, the most notably diverse of which being *Days of Heaven* (1978, Malick), *Robocop* (1987, Verhoeven) and *The Artist* (2011, Hazanavicius). Another of *Phantom of the Paradise*'s crew, costume designer Rosanna Norton, would provide the same service on *Carrie* before going on to work on the likes of *Tron* (1982, Lisberger), *Gremlins 2: The New Batch* (1990, Dante) and *The Patriot* (2000, Emmerich). Similarly, special effects artist Gregory M. Auer returned from *Phantom*, before going on to work on *Star Wars* and *The Hills Have Eyes*.

One of the most important figures in *Carrie*'s transition to the big screen, and to both his and De Palma's future careers, was composer Pino Donnagio. Born into a family of musicians, Donnagio studied the violin from the age of ten and made his solo debut, aged fourteen, during a Vivaldi concert on Italian radio. Having discovered popular music, Donnagio would sing with Paul Anka before establishing himself as one of Italy's foremost singer-songwriters. Donnagio was, like Spacek in *Carrie*'s lead role, not who De Palma originally had in mind for the job of scoring the film. Given his scores for *Sisters* and *Obsession*, and the director's by now overt identification with Hitchcock, veteran composer Bernard Herrmann was De Palma's first choice. But when Herrmann died, the director turned to the Italian Donnagio, composer of 'Lo Che Non Vivo' ('You Don't Have to Say You Love Me'). Still relatively inexperienced in film composing, with *Don't Look Now* (1973, Roeg) and two small scale Italian movies his only credits thus far, Donnagio would produce a striking mix of tense Herrmannesque/Hitchcockian strings, gentle motifs and pop songs that aurally interpreted De Palma's visual interpretation of King's written material. De Palma himself incorporated Herrmann's stabbing violin motif from *Psycho*'s shower scene into the film's soundtrack, used in the early scenes where Carrie displays her burgeoning telekinetic powers. Donnagio's background in both classical and contemporary music would be reflected in his invocation of the alternating emotions of the cast, the film's tonal shifts (from dramatic to reflective and from romantic to comedic and horrific) and, perhaps most significantly, in compounding tension during the prom night massacre. So complimentary was Donnagio's music to De Palma's images that the composer would become one of the director's most frequent collaborators, providing the scores for, amongst others, *Dressed to Kill* and *Blow Out*.

CARRIE'S WORLD: THE PRINCIPAL LOCATIONS

Principal photography on *Carrie* began on 17 May 1976 and wrapped early in July of the same year. The production was based in and around Los Angeles, California. Interior sets for the White household and the prom massacre scene were built on soundstages at Culver Studios, California and were used in conjunction with several actual locations to bring Carrie White's hermetic universe to life. Jack Fisk, tasked with scouting suitable locations for the movie, drew from his memories of studying in Philadelphia of what are colloquially called 'Father, Son & Holy Ghost houses' in the city to help in his search for a property that could be used for the exterior of the White household. Philadelphia's Trinity houses, to give them their official name, date back to the eighteenth century and generally consist of three small rooms, set out over two or three floors connected by a tight, winding staircase. Built originally to house the poor, with nineteenth century Catholic residents first giving the houses their soubriquet, the properties eventually became much sought after, sometimes being knocked together by wealthy buyers to form larger 'quantities'. Fisk's recollections of these simple, peculiarly Philadelphian residencies were utilised for the set design of the interior of the White household, one that De Palma insisted should be *'infused with a religious fever'*.[6]

The pared back, condensed architectural interior style of the Trinity houses, and the strong, historic links to Catholic communities, were an obvious fit for a household that was to be oppressively dominated by religious paraphernalia. The archaic architectural design of the Trinity house solidifies the movie's placing of Margaret and Carrie White as being out-of-step within their contemporary environment. De Palma's use of doubles or inverted mirror images of characters, themes and environments sees the White household (and by design its occupants) – claustrophobic, unwelcoming and archaic – juxtaposed to symbolic effect with that of the Snell family and their residence – spacious, bright and modern. The continual deployment of doubles and inverted mirror images throughout the narrative is used overwhelmingly to symbolise the split personality of, and the resulting emotional turmoil bubbling away within, Carrie White. The dichotomous interiors of the White and Snell households are visually intrinsic to keeping the carefully designed equilibrium of *Carrie*'s hermetic world intact.

Fisk's location scouting missions eventually led him to 124 N 7th Street, Santa Paula, California. The property's asymmetrical facade, with two windows of unequal size on the ground floor and one centrally positioned window on the top floor gave the White household an off-kilter exterior that symbolised the out-of-whack inner environments of its residents. Standing, at the time, next to a vacant lot also helped in the decision to use the property, allowing as it did easy access for the production's crew to obtain the required shots.

Filming for the movie's other main location – Bates High School – took place at Palisades Charter High School, Pacific Palisades, LA and at Pier Avenue Junior High School, in Hermosa Beach, CA. Pier Avenue Junior High provided the interiors and exteriors of Bates High School while the athletics field at Palisades Charter High School became Bates'. While Pier Avenue Junior High closed the same year that *Carrie* was filmed (it's now the Hermosa Beach Community Center), Palisades Charter High School, established in 1961, is now highly ranked and listed as a California Distinguished School. These establishments, represented onscreen in their physical actuality, were places instantly familiar to a large proportion of *Carrie*'s target audience on a daily basis and familiar from memory at the very least to the cross-generational viewers exposed to the movie. Of course, the emotional terrain traversed within their walls spoke to every generation, an element that King and, especially, De Palma addressed and took to its most extreme outcome.

Fisk gives credit for finding the location used when Billy kills the pig to Bill Paxton, then sometimes employed by Fisk as a scouting assistant. Farmer John's Pig Mural, which surrounds the Farmer John Brand Clougherty Meat Packing Company (now owned by the multinational Hormel Food Corporation), lies five miles south of downtown LA. The striking 4000 square foot artwork, described by art dealer Ivan C. Karp as '*a fundamental tract for West Coast vernacular painting*',[7] was begun by Hollywood set painter Les Grimes in 1957. Bizarrely, Grimes fell to his death while working on the piece in 1968 and mural painter Arno Jordan was hired to complete Grimes' work, add his own touches to it and undertake subsequent restoration work over the coming years. The subject of numerous newspaper and website articles over the years, in De Palma's hands Farmer John's Pig Mural provided an artificially bucolic backdrop to the instigation of Chris' decidedly unnatural plan for Carrie's public humiliation. Brief as its appearance in the movie might be, Farmer John's Mural – a romantic representation of a rural idyll surrounding the grim actuality of a slaughterhouse and industrial meat packing plant – points to so many of *Carrie*'s underlying themes; fantasy and reality, passivity and dominance, kindness and cruelty and innocence and bloody, violent experience. Far from merely being backdrops to the narrative, the principal locations utilised by De Palma play as crucial a role in the narrative as that of its characters. The high school(s), the White and Snell households and the meat packing plant give an aura of verisimilitude to the supernatural and bring symbolism to the everyday.

FOOTNOTES

1.   From the 'Visualizing *Carrie*' documentary extra feature on the 25th anniversary DVD release.
2.   In 'The Greatest Films of All Time', *Sight & Sound*, September 2012, vol 22, issue 9.
3.   From the 'Acting *Carrie*' documentary extra feature on the 25th anniversary DVD release.
4.   See 1.
5.   See 2.
6.   See 1.
7.   Sourced from the 'Pleasure Palate: Tasting Life's Pleasures' blog.

PART 3: *CARRIE*: AN ANALYSIS

*Carrie is so successfully manipulative that its essential callousness is obvious only after its
bravura cinematic impact has worn off.* (Newman, 1988: 124)

Whether or not one agrees with the above statement that *Carrie* is essentially callous,
to my mind there is little argument that De Palma's movie is '*successfully manipulative*'.
The phalanx of critical readings of *Carrie* – be they positive, negative, impassioned or
ambivalent – mark the narrative, and specifically De Palma's visualisation of it, as one
that demands intellectual engagement. The director's stylistic approach to adapting
King's source material is the primary reason that the finished movie has engendered
such a variety of critical reactions as well as its narrative resonating so deeply with
viewing audiences. From its opening volleyball match to its closing shots of a traumatised
Sue being comforted by her mother, *Carrie* is a tightly controlled, rhythmical exercise
in audience manipulation that constantly confounds audience identification and
expectation. Though certain set piece sequences – the shower room sequence, the 'Last
Supper', the prom massacre, Sue's nightmare – offer the clearest avenue for assessing
De Palma's vision of the material and the subsequent critical readings of them, the
film works as a complete narrative because of its integration of gentler, comedic and
romantic sequences. Duality – of scenes, techniques, characters, motifs and symbolic
imagery – is a strong influence throughout, tying together opposing forces, reflecting
alternate viewpoints and periodically reminding the audience that none of the principal
figures are clearly defined 'character types'. Similarly, the dominant text and underlying
subtexts addressed in the complete movie and in its individual sequences reveals how
Carrie can alternately be viewed as pop culture, mythologised horror and politicised
cultural critique. *Carrie* is a movie that instantly succeeds in delivering a blast of
(seemingly throwaway) genre entertainment that on repeated viewings grows richer in
its assemblage and infinitely more caustic in meaning. By looking at its key themes/motifs
and their deployment in specific scenes/sequences, including how themes/motifs bleed
into each other and how scenes/sequences play off each other, a complete appreciation
of De Palma's enduringly resonant movie can be gleaned.

KEY THEMES

Religion

These are Godless times, Mrs. Snell.

Religious belief, of a fanatical Judeo-Christian strain, plays a key role within *Carrie's* narrative. Represented by and through the figure of Margaret White – zealous, repressed and domineering – dogma, literal readings of the Bible, iconography and prayer are primarily deployed as symbolic instruments in the oppression of Carrie White. It is not religion *per se* that comes under attack in the movie but, ironically, the spiritually corrosive dangers inherent in fundamentalist lifestyles. Carrie White is caught in the middle of the dual oppositional forces of faith and reason, torn between her archaic, spiritually dominated home environment and that of the modern, liberal high school. The belief in God, the ultimate patriarchal figure, places Margaret White herself in line with the other central female characters in the movie – Carrie, Sue, Chris and Miss Collins. Not as overtly addressed as the oppression of her daughter, Margaret's subservience to patriarchal authority can be seen in terms of how Carrie *et al* individually respond to their femininity and place within a dominant patriarchal society. Margaret White is both victim and aggressor, as divided as her daughter and equally as tormented. Seen through the eyes of Margaret, sex, alcohol, dancing and even daytime TV are signs of the '*Godless times*' she abhors. A cloud of religious judgement hangs heavy over the themes of sex, family life, authority and womanhood that affect not just Carrie White but her classmates' lives as well. Their apparent straying from God's Word is the sinful path which Margaret so virulently, violently strives to keep her daughter from taking.

For Carrie, growing up in an era of sexual liberation, hedonism and pop culture, the spiritual, and, hence, moral and ethical strains pulling at her psyche are both personal and public. The microcosm environment of Carrie White's home-life is specific to her narrative journey *and* applicable to the macro-cosmic, constantly conflicted emotional journey of the United States, never more apparent than during the era of Free Love, Vietnam, Watergate and Women's Liberation. That religion is used to underpin her oppressive environment is bold and pointed in a country where to this day around 80 per cent of Americans identify with a religious denomination. Despite this, Carrie is a child out-of-time, desperately seeking to be a part of the world around her. It is her mother's repressed emotional state and isolated existence, devoid of anything but The Word of God, projected onto and instilled in Carrie that stifles her and forms one part of her confused, divided personality. De Palma, in his film-making technique, takes the religious theme and integrates it into the camerawork of the film itself. God's eye shots and descending, ascending camera movements are threaded throughout the movie, alternately sitting in judgement from a heavenly position, invading the limbo-like realities of an Earthly purgatory or plunging downwards, as Carrie eventually does, into a Hellish inferno. The Biblical allegories and references are compounded in two pieces of text that appear, one at the beginning of the lengthy prom sequence and the other during the film's coda sequence. A huge sign reading *Love Among the Stars* adorns the upper reaches of the prom venue and the legend *Carrie White Burns in Hell*, accompanied by a helpful downward pointing arrow, is scrawled on the makeshift cross in Sue's nightmare. Simple, even crude, these words and their use may be, but effective within the narrative and the narrative's visual appearance they most certainly are.

The Supernatural

If I concentrate hard enough, I can move things.

The central narrative hook of *Carrie,* the fantastical element that conforms to the traditional horror genre conventions, is telekinesis. Naturally a part of the horror genre since its inception, the supernatural, here specifically supernatural abilities, are powerfully symbolic, destructive elements used to wreak havoc, represent inner turmoil and cross the lines between the known and the unknown. Carrie White's supernatural power is linked to the onset of puberty and menstruation (the physical, tangible counterpart to the supernatural 'other'), a belief drawn from mythology and vividly brought into a contemporary setting. Her budding sexuality and encroaching womanhood are symbolically aligned with the emergence of strange, witch-like powers. Barbara Creed, Vivian Sobchack and Carol Clover paid particular attention to the association of menstruation with supernatural abilities in *Carrie,* and also in *The Exorcist* in Sobchack's case. Creed's 'Woman as Witch: *Carrie*' chapter from *The Monstrous-Feminine; Film, Feminism, Psychoanalysis* (1993) is a significant tract on how the supernatural and menstruation come together in the movie to offer up the reading that Carrie White is a witch, albeit a witch going to school in '70s America. In describing Carrie's and *The Exorcist's* Regan's bleeding as *'an apocalyptic feminist explosion of the frustrated desire to speak'* (1978: 193), Sobchack strikingly highlights how Carrie's increasingly shocking displays of supernatural power eventually give terrifying voice to her life-long, downtrodden frustrations. For Clover, Carrie's apocalyptic display of otherworldly power marks the point where the *'supernatural and psycho-sexual intersect: cause a girl enough pain, repress enough of her rage, and no matter how fundamentally decent she may be, she perforce becomes a witch'* (1992: 71). Rather than condemning Carrie, this points to a fundamental aspect of the psychological make-up of human beings. Pushed to extremes and/or exposed to negative forces for long enough, any one of us is liable to act or react to situations in ways hugely detrimental to ourselves or those around us. *Carrie* may present a wildly fantastical vision of one teenage girl's bastardised coming-of-age, through its employment of supernatural elements, but there is a realist strain underpinning it all.

Carrie's telekinetic abilities also provided De Palma with the perfect outlet for his creative urges, most memorably displayed in the prom night massacre and Carrie's eventual matricide. Carrie's powers are utilised by the director to provide viewers with the cinematic thrills they have come to expect from the genre. That he did so in such symbolic fashion created richly fertile ground for critical discussion, leaving the movie with one foot in pop culture territory and one in the academic camp. In discussing De Palma's body of work, Wood aligns the figure of the director with that of Carrie by stating that *'the artistic personality the films define is that of a fundamentally feminine man who, because he is a man within a patriarchal culture, can view his femininity only in terms of castration'* (Wood, 86: 147). In these terms, and with the director's kinetic style, the explosive destruction witnessed during the prom night massacre becomes as much about the director's issues as it does about Carrie White's. It also gives further credence, if any were needed, to Clover's assertion that the gender of a central character is of little importance in terms of identification. In the course of the movie, Carrie displays traits hitherto traditionally identified with females *and* males as well as an unsettling, unknowable other. Her unfortunate place in the hierarchical order of the high school, barely registering even at the lowest echelons, is a universal experience, either personal or as witness to its corrosive impact on the lives of those deemed 'other'.

Adolescence

All the kids think I'm funny, and I don't wanna be.

The portrait of adolescence in *Carrie* veers between bruising humiliations, comedic escapades, manipulative, sexually driven power-plays and the insecurities fostered by peer pressure. It is a world and a time familiar to us all, a prime reason why coming-of-age movies of all varieties strike such chords with cinema-goers. The coming-of-age narrative woven through *Carrie*'s fabric aligns the movie thematically with others from a multitude of genres; from the French New Wave in *Les Quatre cents coup* (1959, Truffaut), via social realism in *Kes* (1969, Loach) to the independent stylings of *The Last Picture Show* (1971, Bogdanovich) and the mainstream teen comedy of *Mean Girls* (2004, Waters). *Carrie*'s isolating everyday existence and traumatic crossing from naivety to knowing is as profoundly a painful representation of the loneliness, confusion and desperation felt by an adolescent character as cinema has thrown at us. Presented alternately in grimly realistic, lighthearted or operatically fantastical terms, Carrie White's teenage life, and those of Sue Snell, Chris Hargensen, Tommy Ross and Billy Nolan cover the full range of interests, afflictions, pressures and fears experienced by the average adolescent from all walks of life. Where Carrie's specific experience of religious indoctrination may not resonate with the majority of viewers, the confusing, emotionally fraught contradictions between dependence on parental guidance and the safety of the family home and the child's desire to break free of the mental and environmental shackles of that guidance and the family home cannot fail to strike a chord on some level.

Carrie, Sue & Tommy and Chris & Billy, as well as the secondary teenage characters, are representative of personality types drawn from the wellspring of adolescent experience of King, De Palma, Cohen, the cast and, crucially, the audience. Individual characters they may be, but in De Palma's hands their personalities – innocent, experienced, pure, sullied, insecure, homely, sexualised – and their flexible character traits – quiet, shy, dominant, level headed, dysfunctional, delinquent – are divisions of the psyches of each and every one of us. It is through Carrie's tormented struggle to exhibit the popular, seemingly worldly traits adopted by Sue, Chris and the other girls that reflections of our own adolescent struggles, regardless of gender, are evoked. Within a hierarchical peer group (in many ways a mirror image of the adult world the characters are on the cusp of entering) dominated by popularity, bullying, sexual discovery, childish pranks and longed for freedom, Carrie White represents the thing none of us wanted to be, the one marked out as 'different', 'not like us' and 'other'. Part of the horror of the movie is the awareness that Carrie is doomed, the die is cast and the damage inflicted so scarring that salvation for her is impossible. That she takes everyone else down with her is equally as troubling given the horrific rise in acts of violence, revenge driven or otherwise, perpetrated by teenagers on other teenagers (and adults) in contemporary society. Among the movie and the novel's wider implications is that the adult world that waits is one entranced by yet terrified of adolescents, especially female adolescents, just as many in her peer group appear to be by Carrie. Carrie's eventual rejection and destruction of both her peer group and the figures of authority that dominate her world speaks of youthful rebellion run uncontrollably, savagely wild and of the authoritarian/familial/social fears of that happening.

Women

They're called breasts, Momma, and every woman has them.

Carrie is a movie with women at its heart; addressing or evoking femininity, feminism, the 'sisterhood' (a debatable concept) and the place of women under patriarchy. This overt theme has been at the forefront of the reactions to the movie, both at the time and subsequently. De Palma has been openly castigated for apparent misogyny, defended from those barbs by other critics/academics and issues concerning gender identification, sexuality, subservience, dominance, domesticity and body image have all being addressed via the figures of its central female characters. The mothers, daughters, teachers and friends in *Carrie* play off, into and against patriarchal, gender and social expectations. Written, adapted and directed by men, *Carrie* is a divisive movie, existing in various readings as a male vision of a female world, an extreme vision of female liberation, a reaction against the era's shifting gender roles, a bleak view of the 'sisterhood', a gender-free, symbolic tale of revenge or, as I see it, and like Carrie White herself, a blank slate onto which identity is projected.

Splintered like the titular figure's psyche, the representation of females in the movie varies drastically. Margaret, Carrie, Sue, Chris, Miss Collins, Norma and Mrs. Snell between them occupy the position or embody the idea of villain, victim, monster, 'good', 'evil', sacrificial lamb, promiscuity, hedonism, purity, knowledge, authority, ally, foe, passivity, dominance and objectified fantasy figure. The men in their lives – God, absent fathers and husbands, ineffectual authority figures, pliable lovers or inescapable classmates – inhabit a secondary, but contradictory, position in the movie. The world these females inhabit is one constructed and presided over by men; Carrie's menstruation ushers in the possibility of sexual relations with men, Sue and Chris both manipulate, but rely on, their male lovers to carry out their plans, Miss Collins' fondest memory is of her high school prom date, Mrs. Snell is the bored, frustrated housewife whiling her days away with a glass in one hand and television soaps for company and Margaret, abandoned by her husband, is obsessively devoted to a higher power drawn in rigidly masculine terms.

The mother/daughter relationship – symbiotic yet dichotomous – is another of the dual themes/forces running through *Carrie*'s narrative, here rendered in tragic fashion as the 'sins' of the mother, in her eyes, can be seen to be visited upon the daughter. A prominent part of the complete narrative, the mother-daughter relationship is the most complex and contentious element of the movie. The bonds between Margaret and Carrie are presented in 'monstrous' terms, diseased blood ties that aren't even severed by murder, as the act of matricide follows attempted infanticide and leads to the literal collapse of the family home.

The director's complex relationship with women is a vital ingredient in the movie's approach to the representation of females, with Wood arguing that '*De Palma's habitual identification with women is accompanied, paradoxically, by an apparent animus against them, the contradiction often expressing itself in the treatment of a single character*' (1986: 147). Clearly, Carrie White is the '*single character*' applicable to Wood's assertion, but in *Carrie* the female characters surrounding the central figure are fractured images of what Carrie White is, would like to be or is scared of becoming. The cruel female peer group that so belittles Carrie during the catalytic shower room sequence is a damning reflection of the erosion to feminine liberty done by patriarchal expectations, turning as they do on one of their own. Rejecting Carrie for her 'otherness' and failure to match up to their expectations of her, drawn from the male expectation of women projected onto them, 'Carrie becomes acceptable to these same women only when she attends the prom, after she has brought her appearance and behaviour into alignment with their own' (Magistrale, 2003: 29). Being an adolescent female in the world Carrie plays out in, reflective of the one it came out in, is to know that 'all girls have to look forward to under patriarchy... is conforming to mother's image, itself determined by male desire and its attendant discourse' (Humphries, 2003: 96). De Palma's vision of females in Carrie is, to my mind, dominated by duality. Savage yet tender, accusatory and defensive, forgiving and unforgiving and embracing and disavowing, De Palma is not indecisive but rounded in his portrayal. He identifies, for good or ill, much more with females, and by extension adolescents and rebellious anger, in Carrie than in any other of his films before or since.

Authority

You're out of the prom, Hargensen!

No self-respecting movie centered on teenage life would be complete without authority figures for those teenagers to kick against, aspire to be like or try to manipulate for their own ends. The two dominant authority figures in Carrie, Margaret White and Ms. Collins, between them symbolise the Church, the family and the state. The narrative's sealed world can be taken on face value – one troubled girl's descent into barbarity – or seen as a symbolic attack on the institutions placed at the head of and responsible for society and social cohesion. The Church, the family and the state, three institutions at the heart of American social values, are gleefully torn apart by De Palma via Carrie's explosion of vengeful fury. By engulfing the prom venue and the White household in flames, thereby killing those inside, Carrie/De Palma carries out an unbridled, pessimistic attack on the bedrocks of the contemporary society into which they were born. The literal victims may be those that have, and more troublingly haven't, caused her such anguish, but the additional, metaphorical victims – family home and school – are razed to the ground in a clearly confrontational manner. What angst-ridden adolescent, during their wildest, darkest flights of fancy, hasn't imagined such a thing, or something similar to it? For Wood, this is a pivotal conceit of the genre as a whole: 'central to the effect and fascination of horror films is their fulfillment of our nightmare wish to smash the norms that oppress us and which our moral conditioning teaches us to revere' (Wood, 1986: 80).

As a vision of teenage violence perpetrated against peers and authority figures, Carrie White's murderous rampage was prescient and remains disturbing. Neither King nor De Palma could have known that Carrie's acts would be echoed in such distressing fashion in the subsequent years via the unprecedented rise in high school massacres carried out by disturbed pupils. Their combined commentaries on high school life, the corruption of American social values and, specifically, the increasing alienation of the country's youth became shockingly manifest in a number of barbaric acts, of which the Columbine massacre remains the most high profile example. Carrie White may be a fictional composite of wretched figures drawn from the memories of King, De Palma and Spacek, but there is a chilling veracity, now more than ever, to that representation of troubled youth. By centering on the alienated life of an adolescent female, King and De Palma unwittingly second guessed an issue that has been an ever present in American society since: the murderous teen who violently rejects not only their peers, but their authority figures too. What was once just an 'American problem' is now a global one, with similar incidents happening in educational establishments around the world in troublingly frequent numbers. That these atrocities are executed exclusively by males points to a contemporary crisis in both youth and masculinity that is outside of the realm of this study. But if *Carrie* was a dissemination of its era's crisis in femininity and the shifts in the representations of female characters in popular culture, then *The Basketball Diaries* (1995, Kalvert), *Elephant* (2003, Van Sant) and *We Need To Talk About Kevin* (2011, Ramsay) are its contemporary, male-driven siblings. As with many of the horror genre's strongest entries, it is the wider implications of a narrative that add to the movie's weight, and *Carrie*'s representation of authority is as damning as any committed to celluloid. Self-serving, hypocritical, detached and dominant but emotionally weak, authority figures, as they are in the majority of horror movies from the '70s, are to be railed against, ignored, manipulated or attacked, usually fatally.

KEY MOTIFS

Blood

After the blood comes the boys.

Carrie, isolated on the frame, stares in horror at the blood on her hands

Blood oozes from *Carrie*'s every pore; sticking, staining, shaming and spilling from orifices, wounds and buckets for all to see. Vivid in colour (utilised elsewhere in other ways during the movie) and repulsive in its deployment, blood is the catalytic substance that drives the movie. Menstrual blood, that 'curse' visited upon woman, pigs' blood and blood from penetrated bodies symbolically punctuate the narrative; wounds to the psyche, tears in perception and stains on character are given physical form. The provocative use of pig's blood is examined in *The Monstrous Feminine*, with the author connecting *Carrie*'s contemporary milieu to ancient history and beliefs. Creed draws attention to the fact that '*in Greek and Latin the female genitals are referred to as "pig", and the Cowrie Shell, which clearly represents the female genitals was called "pig"*' (1993: 80).[1] Her assertion that '*menstrual blood is constructed as a source of abjection: its powers are so great it can transform woman into any one of a number of fearful creatures: possessed child, killer and vengeful witch*' (ibid: 83) points to the unsettling, 'taboo' challenging nature of the narrative, its historical associations, both actual and fictional, and to the fear and persecution of those deemed other, unclean or cursed. De Palma challenges the viewer, both male and female, to confront the essentially adolescent way in which menstruation is still, to this day, treated in society. We may collectively be more open about discussing this most intimate of bodily functions now than then, but the contemporary one-liner *'how can you trust something that bleeds for five days and doesn't die'* is an indicator of the underlying disquiet that menstruation still evokes in society, if only in the male section of it. As to whether De Palma is attesting that womanhood and menstruation are loathsome and disgusting, MacKinnon shrewdly notes that *'in order to believe that womanhood is a matter of disgust, the viewer must believe that Mrs. White's teaching is right. Carrie explicitly rejects it. Yet several commentators have argued themselves into the position that the film speaks for Mrs. White, not Carrie'* (1990: 125). The audience is given the opportunity to see things from Margaret's perspective, but it is a perspective easily rejected. To allow, or lead, the viewer to occupy the position of a number of characters in the movie is not to lock them in to that position. If that were the case, then the distancing techniques used during Carrie's prom night massacre wouldn't work, and the evident confusion wrought in terms of identification with the central figure are testament to the fact that they do.

Blood is a visual motif, linking the beginning, middle and end of *Carrie*. The onset of the traumatised teenager's menarche leads to the hand-print menstrual bloodstain on Miss Collins' gym shorts that outwardly marks her inner shame at empathising with the bullies, and highlights Principal Morton's discomfort with the whole subject of female menstruation. The slaughter of the pig to provide the means for Carrie's public humiliation later becomes symbolic of a birth, as the drenched Carrie White fully evolves into the 'monstrous feminine' figure before performing a symbolic rebirth by peeling off the prom dress, rendered as an embryonic skin, and cleansing herself. Margaret's bleeding wounds are a physical replica of the inanimate wounds of the statue of St. Sebastian, and, finally, we are left with Carrie's blood stained hand reaching out of the grave to grab onto not just Sue's arm, but her, and our, psyche.

Naturally a frequent sight in horror movies, blood in *Carrie*, through the focus on menstruation, ties in with dialogue riven with references to the body, bodily emissions and sexual acts to form the prototype gross-out narrative. The words 'shit', 'fuck', 'tits', 'suck', 'ass' and 'pussy' flow from the mouths of various characters at regular intervals; profanity deployed as a constant reminder that the body – here youthful and female – is the site of the horror in the movie. Far from being profane for profanity's sake, these spoken instances tie in with Creed's notion that *'images of blood, vomit, pus, shit, etc. are central to our culturally/socially constructed notions of the horrific'* (1993: 13), in a continuation of the themes posited by Julia Kristeva in *Powers of Horror: An Essay on Abjection* (1982). Uncomfortable visual imagery reflected by coarse language is now a mainstay of the teen horror and comedy genres, but in *Carrie* it was bold, confrontational and entirely intrinsic to the narrative. De Palma integrates the colour red – the colour, of course, of blood – into the narrative not just to 'stain' and 'shame' but also to 'mark' characters out for death. Norma's baseball cap, Tommy's pick-up truck and Billy's car are all a striking shade of red, as is Chris' lipstick, seen in the movie's most extreme close-up prior to her pulling the rope that sends the bucket of pigs' blood down onto the unsuspecting Carrie. Red plays an essential role during the prom night sequence itself, both before and after Chris' humiliating stunt, marking out almost all of the assembled guests as well as forming one part of the overriding colour scheme of the sequence – red, white and blue – the colours of the Stars and Stripes.

Shameful, gross, belittling, humiliating and just plain dirty, blood and profanity in *Carrie* repeatedly surface to remind us of the body, its emissions, our conscious or unconscious obsession with them during adolescence and, particularly, how menstrual blood is the source of our greatest collective discomfort, more so than shit, when talking, or joking about, the human body. There are no mutated, Cronenbergian orifices or heavy duty phallic weapons at large in *Carrie*; rather, there is a girl and her pain at a world in which she is on the margins. Even her menstrual cycle, the thing that she shares with all the other females in her peer group, is used as another battering ram with which to ridicule her.

Duality

Oppositional, doubled and reflected characters, scenes, colours, dialogue and camera movements have long been a part of De Palma's method, and *Carrie* is awash with instances of the deployment of duality. With Carrie White as its focal point, the movie bombards both the downtrodden girl and the viewer with a litany of good/evil, light/dark, comedic/horrific, tender/savage and innocent/sullied references, symbols and alternating visions that give balance to its structure, appearance and narrative. In a movie where the central character is torn between who she is and who she wants to be, and, furthermore, between how others see her and how *they* want her to be, De Palma's predilection for duality – think *Sisters* and *Body Double* – found another ideal outlet. The dividing lines are, naturally, blurred in De Palma's hands, lending either a frustrating ambiguity or an honesty about the human condition, depending on one's standpoint regarding the director and his oeuvre. *Carrie*, for this author at least, is horrific precisely because the lines are blurred, as they are in the real world. Carrie White performs a 'monstrous', unforgivable act, but she is herself no 'monster', her destructive rampage is a representation of the cry of anguish buried deep inside every bullied child, boy or girl.

The alternate figures of Margaret White and Miss Collins, and those of Sue Snell and Chris Hargensen, for instance, appear to be clearly defined opposites. Margaret – dour, domineering, cold, archaic – and Miss Collins – bright, authoritative but caring and modern – can be seen, in the crudest terms, as 'bad' and 'good' mothers respectively. The biological 'bad' mother with her wrong-headed parental approach, and the substitute 'good' mother, with her kindly words and nurturing attitude, are versions of the possible adult version of Carrie herself, if she were ever to have reached full maturity. Things aren't so clear cut, though; both women project their own fears, insecurities and aspirations onto Carrie, attempting to mould her from girl to woman in their own images, images that Carrie will fluctuate between before rejecting them both. With little regard for what Carrie might actually want, they push, demand, coax and harangue her into following their wishes, wishes drawn from personal experience and outlook. Their language, appearance and demeanour may be the negative of the other, but the underlying factor in their mental and physical make-ups is the same: life has taught us this, and you will learn from us.

Similarly, Sue and Chris are drawn, on appearances, as the 'good' girl and the 'bad' girl – one with the all American boyfriend and the other with a delinquent lover. Sue, the brunette with the good grades and a conscience and Chris, blonde, loud mouthed and sexually potent, are versions of Carrie that appeal but are beyond her reach, and lie far outside how she is seen by others. Again, De Palma toys with the alternate visions he presents us with. Both Sue and Chris use sex, or the promise of it, to manipulate their boyfriends into aiding them with their respective plans for Carrie. There is no clearly delineated 'good' or 'bad' in the movie, only fluctuating shades of each. Sue may appear to be altruistic in her attempts to make amends to Carrie, but it is shame and guilt that inspires her actions. Though not seen to engage in sexual activity with Tommy (which she does in the novel), the implications are evident that Tommy will be 'rewarded' should he acquiesce to Sue's wishes. The flipside to the scene in which Sue sits in passive-aggressive silence, withholding her 'love', until Tommy agrees to ask Carrie to the prom is an intercut sequence in which Chris, never passive-aggressive, enthusiastically fellates Billy in the front seat of his car, knowing that sexual favours given in advance will be reciprocated with his help in setting up the prom night prank. Tommy and Billy, polar opposites in terms of social standing and future expectations, are pliable material in the hands of their respective partners; dual figures, one driven by 'love' and the other guided by 'lust'. Magistrale breaks down the duality involved in the movie even further, drawing comedy and horror together by stating that 'what Billy Nolan and Chris Hargensen do to Carrie is both cruel and terrifying, but the two of them are hilarious in the process' (Magistrale, 2003: 12). In deconstructing the fellatio scene, he later compounds just how ingrained duality is. As Sue and Tommy calmly sit in silence, the former doing homework the latter watching a movie on the television (marked for death in a bright red jumper), Chris and Billy are a riot of noise, colour and energy. Bad language, playful slaps, alcohol, make-up, rock music and, ultimately, sexual activity render them as the (black) comedians to Sue and Tommy's straight guys. Magistrale pertinently ascertains that the sequence is 'a brilliantly balanced fluctuation between adolescent play and rape, sexual titillation and manipulation, heterosexual attraction and repulsion' (ibid: 26).

Beyond the characters and their actions, Carrie features numerous dual scenes/sequences that complement the narrative, rather than detract or distract from it, an accusation that De Palma has faced throughout his career. The aforementioned sequences in which Sue and Chris inveigle Tommy and Billy into their plans have additional dual-purpose serving sequences dotted around them. During the comedic sequence where the teens prepare for the prom, Carrie is seen trying out lipstick, alone and insecure as Tommy and his pals are trying out suits. They may also be insecure, their bravado masking their own doubts about their appearances; but, crucially, they are together. Carrie looking into her bedroom mirror in a state of anguish, leading to a literally shattered image, is later juxtaposed as Miss Collins gives her a pep talk and beauty tips in a mirror hung in the school. One speaks of the damage to Carrie's internal world, and one to the opportunity to re-invent her physical appearance. As

Carrie is cradled in Miss Collins' arms in the shower room at the movie's outset, so Sue is cradled in her mother's arms at the film's denouement; both out of horror, Carrie from an external emission she has no understanding of and Sue from wounds to her psyche, the cause of which she helped set in motion. This same image of Carrie in a foetal position is replayed and inverted during the movie's cataclysmic ending; where Miss Collins cradles the terrified Carrie, Carrie will later cradle her mother's lifeless body. On each occasion her world comes to an end, one imagined and the other literal, first through her belief that she is dying and latterly as she does so.

De Palma also uses duality to build tension within the narrative, offering an indication of things to come in one brief but telling shot later to be replayed on a vastly grander scale. As Billy Nolan struggles to put the bucket onto the rafters of the prom venue, the torch Chris is holding is splattered by falling droplets of blood. It's not an accidental image, but one specifically designed to forewarn the viewer. Like a voyeur spying on an unsuspecting victim, De Palma invites the audience into Billy and Chris' secretive world. Carrie White is right to be wary of Tommy Ross' prom invitation, but only a selective few know why, the audience among that number. Actions and consequences, death and rebirth, humiliation and retribution: duality unsettles in *Carrie*, never letting the audience clearly align their empathy or revulsion. Margaret White occupies a 'villainous' space, but is she not suffering from her own demons? Is she not so mentally, emotionally and spiritually damaged as to be worthy of pity? Aren't Chris, the 'bitch', and Billy, the 'stupid shit', lovable rogues despite their actions? Do we not mourn the deaths of everyone, including the cabal of bullies that have made Carrie White's life so painful?

The *Psycho* strings

Discordant, anguished and referential, the stabbing strings that rupture the movie's aural landscape coincide with the supernatural's fracturing of the 'real world'. The string motif, an obvious nod to Herrmann's work on *Psycho*, is a musical representation of telekinesis, of the flexing (a word repeatedly used in the novel) of Carrie's mind and of terror being visited upon those onscreen. An unmelodious catchphrase, the stabbing strings punctuate the movie at regular intervals as Carrie White's otherness erupts into view. Pino Donnagio's score is interrupted by the aural motif in tandem with the moments that her latent telekinetic abilities interrupt Carrie's 'normal' life. These interruptions gradually increase and finally explode during the prom night sequence with such force that the screen splits in two.

The motif speaks of the control De Palma instils on proceedings, of the integration of imagery, dialogue and sound and of the effect Carrie's powers have on the movie itself. When watching *Carrie* it is evident that it is not just the characters or environments that are attacked, but the screen and the soundtrack also. The motif isn't there as a casual addendum, it is there to complement and reflect. The multiple uses of split-dioptre, a lens filter which gives two clear images in one, and split-screen, which literally divides the image, are fractures to the screen, as the motif is to the soundtrack, as telekinesis is to normality. Carrie White's powers invade her body, the onscreen world, the eyes that see it and the ears that hear it. Carrie becomes, as she does during the prom night massacre, an unstoppable, larger-than-life force, and the repeated use of the aural motif leads us to the point where the screen splits in two, as her psyche finally cracks and the 'other', the 'monstrous feminine', is released. A pointer to a tearing of the fabric of reality, Carrie's and the audience's perception of it and the movie's representation of it, the aural motif is a part of Carrie White's unconscious. A piercing, unpleasant sound, it is the sound of adolescent fury stirring, of worlds colliding and of the return of the repressed.

Split images

As De Palma gave voice to the supernatural with the stabbing strings, he uses split-dioptre and split-screen to isolate within the frame, portray Carrie's fractured mind and even to draw comparisons between characters. Stylistic tics associated with the auteurist director, split-dioptre and split-screen shots in *Carrie* serve an integral purpose to the narrative. The multiple split-dioptre scenes distance one character from another, or others, and, just as the narrative does, draws attention from one vision to another within a single mise-en-scène. Carrie, her mother, Miss Collins and Tommy Ross are all foregrounded in split-dioptre sequences for different reasons. Carrie stands out but is invisible in contradictory fashion as she waits outside Principal Morton's office, large in the frame but insensitively ignored as the authority figures loudly discuss the shower room incident. Margaret White sits impassively in the foreground as Carrie stands

One of numerous uses of split-dioptre lenses in the movie

furtively in the background, Margaret distant, cold and dominant while seated only a few feet away from her child. Miss Collins aggressively puts the girls through their detention workout, her charges collectively occupying the rear of the image, the teacher solely at the front. She is separated by status but associated by guilt, her own shame at empathising with the girls already examined in the earlier split-dioptre office scene. Miss Collins is different but the same, hurtling unknowingly towards the same fate as that of her charges.

In Tommy Ross' case, the use of split-dioptre draws him into Carrie's world while establishing comparisons between the two. During the English class in which Carrie declares Tommy's (copied) poem to be 'beautiful', the young jock's face is shown in stark close up, with the whole of Carrie occupying the right side of the rear of the image. It's an explicit link in more ways than one; as well as her mother, Tommy fills Carrie's mind, fear replaced by yearning. They are both fresh faced, blond/e and distinctive, and Tommy will become the unwitting bait that leads Carrie to her most public humiliation. Within one image, by the use of split-dioptre, De Palma therefore visually propels the narrative, establishes the place of characters within that narrative and defines the personalities of those characters. He may twist, dismantle or contradict those personality traits and the characters places within the movie in due course, but the bedrocks are laid for him to do so by the employment of this stylistic trope.

The appearance of a split-screen sequence in *Carrie* is of no surprise to those familiar with De Palma's movies, as they have been utilised on a regular basis. However, in the

'Visualizing *Carrie*' DVD documentary extra feature, De Palma expresses dissatisfaction with the use of split-screen in depicting the beginning of Carrie's murderous rampage, saying that it is too gimmicky and not visceral enough for action sequences and going so far as to call it a 'great mistake'. The man himself may not be convinced by its use, but the split-screen sequence works in other ways if not in conveying action. Symbolic of her mind being rent asunder, the screen divides in two as the monster within takes control. Both witness and perpetrator, Carrie White takes swift, brutal revenge on those around her. The split-screen sequence allows De Palma to show the massacre from more than one perspective and distance the viewer from the central, now monstrous, figure. It is an alienating device, this time deployed to alienate the viewer, to throw their empathy with Carrie into troubling waters. There is no escape from the twin pronged images of death and destruction that fill the divided screen. De Palma, at his starkest and cruelest, is saying 'this is what's been coming all along, you knew it, so here it is'. Though the images themselves are singular in nature – retributive violence – the duality here is in the doubling of the image within the frame, and De Palma colours these images blood red as the vengeful tragedy unfolds.

THE OPENING SEQUENCE

Hey, Norma, Carrie's got her period!

By the end of the opening sequence, split in true De Palma fashion into two separate scenes, Carrie White is lying naked, bleeding, humiliated and utterly terrified. She has been slapped with a baseball cap, verbally belittled, told she eats shit, started her first period, laughed at, shied away from, bombarded with sanitary towels and tampons and slapped again. It is cruel, discomforting and bold. It has also been titillating, humdrum, voyeuristic, sensual, romanticised and supernatural. De Palma entices, challenges, toys, alienates and wrong-foots the viewer with imagery, dialogue, sound and technique in a way that squarely establishes the hermetic world the narrative exists in, while introducing the elements that will drive it on to its tragic conclusion. Fantasy is rudely interrupted by reality, as Carrie's menstrual blood interrupts the flow of water, calm is rattled out of slumber by chaos and the rose-tinted spectacles are wiped clean to reveal cold, stark cruelty. Worlds are constructed and demolished in minutes around the titular figure, as the two-faced nature of the characters mirror the duplicitous appearance of the movie itself. E. Peretz (2008), David Greven (2008) and Dmetri Kakmi (2000) have all looked at the director's oeuvre, the movie as a whole and/or *Carrie*'s opening sequence in detail, illuminating the view of how the director addresses the narrative and its visual construction. As ever with De Palma, no-one and nothing is as it seems even from the earliest shots of *Carrie*, the outcome of which is an opening gambit that has spawned critical reactions that passionately decry or celebrate De Palma's visualisation of Carrie White's physically and emotionally painful humiliation. A second version of the shower room scene exists in which the full frontal nudity is toned down, with those previously naked girls now at least half-dressed. This version, shot for and shown on TV only a few times, is an interesting addendum to the movie's history: highlighting as it does the provocative and confusing nature of the scene and the movie generally. While bare breasts and pubic regions, especially those of high school students, were still a little too outre for television at the time, the movie's cruel humiliations and violence, however, were perfectly acceptable home viewing.

Carrie opens as a volleyball match during a high school gym class reaches match point, the opening, blood red, credits continuing to run onscreen. From an omnipotent position in the Gods, the camera slowly descends to single out the figure of Carrie White, standing at the back of the court apart from her teammates and now isolated in the frame. The ball flies past her flailing arms and the match is lost, much to her fellow team members' chagrin. Glum faced and awkward of stance, Carrie is stared at angrily, slapped with a baseball cap and told by a girl that '*you eat shit*'. Cut to the inside of the girls' locker room (a domain prohibited to half the population), as wistful, romantic music plays over silent images of half-dressed or nude teenage girls (at least in the diegesis, if not the actual ages of the actors). The camera tracks past breasts, buttocks and pubic regions in lingering slow motion, a masturbatory fantasy in extremis. Moving through the haze of shower mist the camera nestles onto the naked, again isolated, body of Carrie White, caressing and soaping herself in blissful innocence. Dropping the soap to the floor, Carrie notices a steam of blood trickling down her inner thigh. The music stops, the movie flips back into real time and the diegetic sound returns as the girl, apparently ignorant of menstruation, looks on in terror at the blood seeping through her fingers. The camera follows Carrie as she runs towards the now fully clothed girls, naked, bleeding and crying out for help. Disgusted but amused, the girls circle, jostle and begin to harangue Carrie. Mass laughter counters a lone voice of horror as the naked girl is peppered with sanitary towels and tampons, with the chant of 'plug it up' filling her ears. Crouching like a foetus in the corner of the showers, Carrie is slapped out of her hysteria by the gym teacher, Miss Collins, which coincides with an overhead light bulb exploding. Sending the quietened girls out of the locker room, Miss Collins comforts the terrified girl.

The apparently humdrum volleyball match scene is in actuality a symbolic prelude to the movie's most famous/infamous moment – the bucket of pigs' blood falling onto Carrie – and to its technical/narrative theme of descent from a Heavenly position, via a purgatorial ground level one to a hellish low point. Things descend in *Carrie* with alarming regularity – the camera, volleyball, soap, menstrual blood, Carrie herself, sledgehammer, ribbon (before the bucket), the bucket of pigs' blood, the beam that kills Miss Collins and, finally, the White household's roof. Movement is intrinsically linked to narrative; it is inevitable, as is Carrie's tragic fate. Peretz, in his highly philosophical reading of De Palma's oeuvre, and specifically in this instance about the volleyball match, contends that '*the camera's movement, which followed the ball until its fall, arrests on Carrie's face at precisely the same moment she misses the ball and decides the game's outcome*' (Peretz, 2008: 30). Everything that descends is related to Carrie and the prank at the prom that will trigger her explosion of supernatural revenge, initially signposted by the simple act of the camera descending to rest on her downbeat face. By missing her shot, Carrie decides the fate of the match, as she will later decide the fate of the lives of those around her.

While not being 'horror' in its strictest terms – albeit featuring one brief 'uncanny' moment; the exploding light bulb – the locker room sequence is undoubtedly 'horrific', for Carrie and the viewer, male or female. Carrie's humiliation and her alienated position among her peers, visually established by the isolating of Carrie in the frame on three instances – the final volleyball shot, her sensual, pre-menstrual showering and her cowering in the corner of the showers – is distasteful in the extreme. Her awkwardness, innocence and ignorance are defined by Spacek's adroit use of contrasting facial expressions – from downcast frustration, through sensual pleasure to confusion, anxiety and outright terror. Carrie White is introduced to the viewer in no uncertain terms – she is 'other', but she is *an* 'other' that we recognise and can empathise with. We know from the outset of the film that she is rejected, ridiculed and despised by her peers. Carrie's reaction to the onset of her menarche is pitiful, mystifying and wholly demolishes the titillating vision of the secret world of the girls locker room De Palma momentarily constructed.

The sequence/movie is voyeuristic not simply for pleasure's sake, as Robert Nepoti, author of *Brian De Palma*, contends, but it is so as Carrie is a mirror that reflects society's increasingly dog-eat-dog mentality and the director's view of the inherent peep-show nature of cinema itself. To see the sequence/movie as misogynistic is to misunderstand De Palma and rob the narrative of its dual, duplicitous qualities. The dreamlike quality of the first part of the locker room sequence alludes to it being a sexualised, male-fantasy vision, unlike the mundane realities of post-exercise students showering and changing before their next lesson. The camera lingers over the exposed bodies of the teenagers under false pretenses, one half of a dual image whose latter reverse will shatter the former. The low level lighting, slow motion camera and Donnagio's genteel score evokes soft-core pornography, again to seduce before the introduction of real time camerawork, diegetic sound and unpleasant, deeply un-erotic behaviour. One need only compare *Carrie*'s locker room sequence with the similar one in Danny Steinmann's *Savage Streets* (1984) to see the difference between shooting the female body in order to challenge the audience and propel the narrative and exploiting the female body in a manner that undermines the movie's narrative and production. A rape-revenge movie starring Linda Blair, *Savage Streets*' locker room sequence lingers on soaped up breasts, pubic regions and naked buttocks for no apparent reason other than to titillate. Steinmann exhibits either a pitiful misunderstanding of his own movie's narrative concerns or contempt for them. Watching *Savage Streets* is to watch misogyny masquerading as female empowerment, while watching *Carrie* is to be engaged intellectually in conversation with a director who never shows you something purely for its own sake.

Kakmi, who likens the shower-room sequence to Neoclassical artist Jean-August Dominique Ingres painting *The Turkish Bath* (1862), pertinently reminds us of other barbarous activity by pointing out that the:

...innocent sensuality of the girls in naked play is irrevocably shattered when they turn into a raving pack and metaphorically stone Carrie with sanitary napkins. It's a brutal reality check from which we never recover, and it reminds us of the theme of duplicity at the heart of De Palma's oeuvre.[2]

De Palma first caresses and then slaps the audience in a reverse of Carrie being abused by the girls and then comforted by Miss Collins. This is the male gaze being employed and then deconstructed; the horror visited upon Carrie by her female peers is enacted upon male viewers by De Palma. De Palma aligns himself with his central character and subverts the male gaze by drawing parallels between Carrie's peers' actions and patriarchy's often oppressive treatment of women. Beauty undergoes uglification, that which is appealing becomes something to be repulsed by. No-one is 'innocent' in his eyes or in the narrative, however, as the pack-like mentality of the girls, and their reaction to Carrie's reaction to her first period, is as uncomfortable for females as the switch from sexualised fantasy to de-eroticised stark reality is for males. The introduction of the 'uncanny' into the sequence, through the light bulb exploding, gives the movie its first glimpse of the supernatural.

That telekinesis is linked to the onset of Carrie's menstrual cycle, thereby linking female sexuality to the onset of unusual power, was explored in some detail by Creed. The author uses a section from Heinrich Kramer's 1486 treatise on witchcraft, *Malleus Maleficarum*, to aid her examination of the character of Carrie White being a continuation of the representation of witches in cinema. The full quote reads:

> What else is woman but a foe to friendship, an unescapable punishment, a necessary evil, a natural temptation, a desirable calamity, a domestic danger, a delectable detriment, an evil of nature, painted with fair colours. (1993: 75)

As horrendously misogynistic as these lines are, one cannot help but conjure up the image of Carrie while reading it. In the movie, Carrie divides friends, is her mother's 'punishment', leads Tommy to his death through temptation, shatters the 'family' image, is portrayed as a force of nature and is painted in fair colours by her pink prom dress. But while fitting into this reading of her character, Carrie is not definitively assigned as a 'witch', and certainly not assigned as naturally 'evil' by gender. MacKinnon suggests that *'the question is not so much whether the claimed link between female sexuality and strange power exists, but whether that link is sinister'* (1990: 125). There is an ambivalence present throughout *Carrie* regarding the titular character's telekinetic (read: sexual) power that refutes any reading of the movie where Carrie, and hence female sexuality/womanhood, is portrayed as inherently wicked or sinful. Carrie White *wants* to be 'normal', to fit in, and is driven to exercise the powers that she herself does not fully comprehend only after being placed under extreme duress.

This author subscribes to the view offered up by Greven that:

> De Palma's depiction of women has often been misunderstood. He doesn't exude a misogynistic hatred towards them – far from it. Rather, his position towards them is one of rivalrous and ambivalent identification. He empathizes with their position in patriarchy, affirms and identifies with their desire to transgress against its strictures, especially in matters of sexuality, and then – for the mingled reasons of his pessimism and his profound ambivalence – pulls back to watch the ramifications of their intransigence, often dire if not utterly fatal.[3]

DETENTION

Stick 'em up your a...

One of a number of sequences devoid of any traditional 'horror' elements (though physical exercise employed as punishment is horrific for some), the girls' detention with Miss Collins' evolves from light-hearted, familiar school experience into violent confrontation. In many ways a classic De Palma scene, beginning as one thing and descending into another, the sequence plays authority, rebellion, subservience, the female body, violence and shame off each other to drive the narrative arc towards its subsequent conclusion. Immediately prior to this sequence is a scene in which Miss Collins addresses the wrong-doers in order to spell out the terms of their punishment. For obvious reasons Carrie is absent from the group, excluded by her victimhood. De Palma uses this moment to further instill the teenager's sense of isolation and alienation by showing her gazing in to the gym where the girls are assembled, separated from them in literal terms by the window through which she peers. It is a shot that will be mirrored when Tommy Ross visits the White household and cajoles Carrie into accepting his offer of a date to the prom. Though Carrie opens the main door to the house, she remains behind the outer screen door, still separated from one of her peers, ergo still separated from 'normality'.

The detention sequence features an uptempo, slightly comedic pop melody by Donnagio, repeated during the scenes where Carrie hunts for lipstick and the boys try on tuxedos. De Palma's camera fixates on the teenage girls' bodies as Miss Collins puts them through their paces with a series of star jumps, press ups and jogging on the spot exercises. This isn't fixation on the female form for erotic purposes though; it is because no other form of punishment would have made sense to the narrative. Serafina Kent Bathrick protests that '*De Palma's tracking camera moves past the sweating girls lined up for their punitive workout and records their puffing chests and tired thighs with the same relish he had displayed for the locker room vision*'.[4] It may be done with 'relish' as Bathrick suggests, but the relish has more to do with setting up the scene in order that its tonal shift has greater impact. The girls have punished Carrie for her ignorance of female biology and her own body and Miss Collins punishes the girls by making them exercise their bodies. The three days suspension first mooted is jettisoned in favour of a more fitting penance – run of the mill activity transformed into symbolic recompense. The high school gross-out comedy, horror or horror-comedy has the teenage body and its functions, abuses and sexual orifices at their hearts, and De Palma's inclusion of this sequence prefigures these physical themes. Whether the bodies on show are overweight, spindly, curvy or athletic is of no importance, it is that they are being pushed to their limits by authority that is the key issue.

It is via Chris' growing fury at being made to attend an ostensible boot-camp that the confrontation between authority and youthful rebellion emerges. Shifting from a split-dioptre shot with Miss Collins in the foreground and the increasingly angry and physically exhausted girls in the background, signaling a shift in tone, the camera focuses on Chris as she finally cracks and approaches her tormentor. On being told there are still minutes of the detention period remaining, Chris exclaims '*stick 'em up your a...*', catching herself before finishing the sentence. The challenge to authority has been thrown down, however, and Miss Collins, in this most physical of films, responds by landing a ferocious slap to the side of Chris' face. It is a shocking and telling moment; Miss Collins' loss of control, compounded as she threatens to knock Chris down, speaks of an underlying anger between the generations and of the teacher's self-loathing for initially sharing in the girls' bemusement and revulsion at Carrie's behaviour in the shower room. Gone is the comedic soundtrack and focus on the girls' punishment, interrupted by the quelling of insurrection by physical violence. It ends with Chris' expulsion from the prom. For someone as obsessed with social status and privilege as Chris, this is an act of open warfare, with Miss Collins' literally heavy-handed approach to confrontation ultimately one more step on the road to Carrie's public humiliation – and beyond.

THE LAST SUPPER

I'm going, Momma, and there's nothing you can do to stop me.

The Whites framed as a religious tableaux

The power play between mother and daughter, part of the diseased symbiotic nature of Margaret and Carrie's relationship, undergoes a significant shift when the subject of the forthcoming prom is raised. Spirited, youthful rebellion and tainted parental misgivings clash over supper, the last that mother and daughter will share, in one of *Carrie's* many two hander sequences. At opposite ends of a dinner table, but metaphorically light years apart, Carrie and her mother joylessly eat that most American of desserts, apple pie. Under a depiction of The Last Supper, Carrie announces that she has been asked to the prom by Tommy Ross. This simple statement ushers in the parting of the ways for mother and daughter. In a moment as shocking as it is cruel, Margaret douses Carrie with a cup of tea, inadvertently but symbolically also snuffing out the candle light between them. Margaret's horrified reaction to Carrie's offer of a date is a polar opposite to the motherly happiness one would expect to be evoked in normal circumstances. Pouring forth a stream of Biblical invective, Margaret's oppressive attitude is complemented by the dour, low key lighting and religious iconography that make up the tight mise-en-scène. Margaret's otherworldly faith is met by Carrie's otherworldly abilities, though, as youth defies authority, daughter rejects mother and power overwhelms belief. The horror for the audience in seeing a mother throw a hot drink over her child, a grimly realistic act of parental abuse, is superseded by Margaret's horror at seeing Carrie's 'witch-like' powers on display.

Carrie has incrementally edged away from under her mother's protective wings subsequent to her traumatic shower-room experience, with Margaret's decision to keep her daughter in the dark about menstruation engendering as much distrust in her as she feels towards her peers. Her physical transformation from child to adult sparks a mental desire to play catch up with her body, a spark tightly linked into her emerging sexuality and supernatural gift. During this sequence, in which Carrie's supernatural powers are seen to flourish in their strongest terms up to this point, it is Margaret who becomes trapped in the house with Carrie, where for so long it has been the reverse. If Margaret is frightening because of her fundamentalist beliefs and cruel parental behaviour, Carrie is equally so with her supernatural abilities. This sequence may not have garnered the critical attention given over to the opening scenes, the prom night massacre, Margaret's death or Sue's nightmare, but it is a crucial tipping point in the movie's narrative arc. Carrie *has* to defy her mother's wishes, as all teenagers have to defy their parents at some point in order to blossom into adulthood. The irony in *Carrie* is that Margaret's fears for her daughter, however extremely they may be presented, will eventually come to full fruition. Mother may know best, but here mother is a connecting dot in the long line of figures and incidents that lead to those fears being borne out. The omnipotent viewer watches the dichotomous figures with an awareness of both positions; we want Carrie to stand up to her mother and take a step towards independence, but we know that Margaret's worries are well founded. This does not, however, mean that Margaret's position within the narrative is the one the audience occupies or most readily identifies with. It also does not mean that she is right in her assumption that '*they're all gonna laugh at you*', as they only do so from Carrie's shattered perspective, as evidenced by the kaleidoscopic P.O.V. shot subsequent to her being drenched in blood. We know Margaret is right to be fearful, but we also understand that she is right for the *wrong reasons*. It is her maniacal efforts to prevent Carrie from fully participating in what is considered to be 'normal' life that will have her daughter running towards it, coupled with the audience's knowledge of Chris' plans for her – plans that mother and daughter could in no way be aware of – that positions the viewer in an omnipotent, but powerless, position.

PROM NIGHT

The Devil's got a hold of your soul.

It's no accident that the predominant colour scheme of the entire prom night sequence, from Tommy and Carrie's arrival at the venue to Carrie's fiery departure, matches that of Old Glory. The movie's centrepiece sequence, during which Carrie's incredible 'gift' fully blossoms, gave De Palma carte blanche to utilise almost every trick in his directorial box of tricks and perpetuate a savage demolition job on one of the nation's most cherished collective experiences. When Carrie White deploys her awesome powers in revenge for her public humiliation, De Palma employs the narrative to attack the very heart of an American institution, turning one part of the American Dream into a full blown nightmare.

Dating back to the late 1800s, and initially the preserve of the elite, the prom had become a national rite of passage in American life by the 1950s (the era when the 'teenager' became a clearly delineated demographic), one romanticised step on the road to adulthood . Such is its place in the social calendar of American teenage life, prom night has cemented its place in pop culture. A raft of movies, including *Back to the Future* (1985, Zemeckis), *Prom Night* (1980, Lynch), *Drive Me Crazy* (1999, Schultz) and *Mean Girls*, the 1999 speculative fiction anthology *Prom Night* (edited by Nancy Springer) and the subversive song *Prom Night* by singer/DJ/model Jeffree Star are just some of the instances of prom night appearing in cultural works. The pertinent point in regards to *Carrie* is that the vast majority of popular culture relating to prom night appeared subsequent to its release. Alternative proms, anti-prom proms, adult proms and themed prom parties, not to mention the rise of their importance to the school experience around the world, all indicate that however it is viewed, prom night is an intrinsic aspect of adolescent life, the memories of which are passed on generation to generation. An event that can cost the average family over one thousand dollars and generates multi-million dollar business for a broad range of services – limo hire, flowers, dresses, alcohol, condoms – prom night symbolically marks the end of one's teenage life and the beginning of adulthood. The twist for the majority of the prom guests in *Carrie*, of course, is that the prom becomes the end of their short lives, period. The horror is visceral and without mercy. Teenagers and adults alike become the scapegoats of the scapegoat, the guilty and the innocent are condemned onscreen and off, as Carrie White and Brian De Palma – one vengefully, one gleefully – tear down the walls of an American institution.

Over twenty five minutes in length (almost a third of the movie's entire running time), the prom night sequence is a highly stylised descent from romantic fantasy to supernatural horror via grim, naked reality. De Palma throws everything into the sequence and at the viewer; ascending/descending camerawork, tracking shots, montage editing, extreme close ups, visual metaphors, 360 degree pans, slow motion, split-screen, isolated audio and P.O.V. shots, the aforementioned symbolic colour schemes and complementary diegetic and non-diegetic sound. Bravura and excessive, the sequence, not without its critics (De Palma among them), elicits empathy for, then revulsion at, its central figure and tragic sympathy for her victims, even those who take delight in her humiliation. That those figures are actually limited to Chris, Billy and Norma while Carrie believes it to be everyone who witnessed her repulsive humiliation is key to De Palma's manipulation of audience identification. At this senior prom adolescence is left in ashes, adulthood is judged and found wanting and to be human is to be monstrous; a brutal indictment of society, its conventions and humanity. Though not the actual climax of the movie, it is the end in many ways; of Carrie's fantasy of social acceptance, Miss Collins' and Sue's projected aspirations for her, the family lives of the assembled guests, the town's next generation and any hope of a happy ending for the movie and the viewer.

Following her arrival at the school gymnasium, now transformed into a glittering wonderland heralded by a sign reading 'Love Among The Stars' (religiously symbolic, as it equates to a 'Heavenly' state that Carrie yearns to attain) high up on the building's facade, Carrie is ushered into a world of social acceptance, romance and blossoming confidence. A long, high angled tracking shot takes in the whole of the gymnasium, the prom guests a throng of reds, whites and blues under dangling stars and accompanied by the sounds of a band playing on the stage. The horror for the viewer is that we know this scene and Carrie's night is doomed to end, at the very least, with her fantasy exposed in the cruelest of ways. The tension, horror and helplessness evoked by the sequence increases rather than dissipates with subsequent viewings. However much we may wish for a happy ending, wish for someone else, anyone else, to be named prom King & Queen, Carrie and Tommy will always make that fateful walk up onto the stage where he will actually die and she will figuratively experience another death; hers being social, aspirational and romantic. It is doubly cruel as Carrie is, to some degree, accepted, romanced and in full bloom – one of the girls complements Carrie on her dress, Miss Collins is evidently convinced her morale-raising chat has paid dividends and Tommy is attentive, charming and protective. It is only later, after the blood rains down, that she finds/imagines herself rejected by her peers once again.

De Palma never lets the fantasy settle 100 per cent, though; Norma's instinctive, mocking laughter and the bemused looks of a number of the other prom-goers reminds Carrie and us that this is no 'normal' prom date: the jock and the outcast, the Adonis and the ugly duckling just don't go together in reality, only in the la-la land of the movies and popular fiction does this happen, and De Palma and the viewer know this too. The band are an aural back up to the moments where cruel reality prod at the edges of fantasy, the line '*the Devil's got a hold of your soul*', not only a humorous pop-culture reference to the fears of the moral majority regarding contemporary music and its supposed corrupting influence on the young, but a forewarning to the viewer of the monstrous acts that Carrie will later commit. The religious references culminate in Tommy's insistence of '*to the Devil with false modesty*', when Carrie is initially reluctant to vote for themselves as the prom King & Queen. There could be an accusation that narcissism plays a part in Tommy's downfall here, but given that the voting has been rigged by Chris and her minions it's a difficult reading to sustain with any great conviction. *Carrie* may, as Newman states, be '*essentially callous*', but in Tommy Ross there is a figure that elicits a sympathy as deep as any fostered for Carrie White. He may initially agree to take Carrie to the prom so as to please Sue, but once in her company he is instinctively drawn to the shy, awkward girl at his side. If any of the characters in the movie deserve to be labeled as 'good', it must surely be Tommy Ross? In a flipping of the shower room sequence, the 'fantasy' here is shown at normal speed, with slow motion kicking in as the dream descends into a nightmare. Carrie's giddy, dream-like feelings are given a technical representation, however, as she dances with her Prince Charming, but again it sees De Palma toy with the reality of what they experience and we see.

A technique De Palma used previously in *Obsession* and latterly in *Body Double*, the 360 degree rotating shot, less an *homage* to the similar scene in *Vertigo* and more a cross-movie continuation of themes and their representations, is employed in *Carrie* to compound Carrie and Tommy's whirlwind romance, presented in literal terms. In doing so, it also highlights the highly subjective nature of her perception, with Tommy and Carrie spinning in one direction and the camera circling them in the other. As the song's lyrics ('*I never dreamed someone like you could love someone like me*') accompany them, Carrie and Tommy are caught up in and carried away by the moment, a glittering mirror-ball and twinkling, dangling stars adding to the fantasy construction. It's a moment of pure cinematic bravado from the director, but one that richly captures the 'loss of control' Carrie and Tommy experience at that moment; inner fantasy rendered in visually fantastic terms. It is also one half of a pair of 'loss of control' shots, the other being the immediately more terminal vision of Chris and Billy spinning to their deaths as Carrie flips Billy's car, causing it to repeatedly turn 360 degrees before exploding. The sight of Carrie, Tommy, Chris and Billy spinning wildly within the frame marks them out for death in the same manner as the jock's red jumper, the delinquent's red sports car and the teacher's bloodstained shorts.

When Tommy and Carrie are named the prom King & Queen De Palma flips the action into slow motion, this time heralding the intrusion of the harsh reality that shatters Carrie's dream-like state. Lasting a full five minutes from the moment Tommy and Carrie leave their table to the initiation of Carrie's blood drenched, bug-eyed vengeance, DePalma dispenses with dialogue, relying on visual story-telling constructed through editing, audience foreknowledge and the manipulation of the principal characters' points of view. Carrie, Chris, Sue and Miss Collins are the eyes and ears of the audience throughout the slow motion set-piece: Carrie sees her dreams apparently come true,

As Carrie's psyche finally splits, so does the screen, an oft used technique by De Palma

Chris relishes the power of bringing Carrie's dream to an end with almost orgasmic delight, Sue tries in vain to stop the humiliation and Miss Collins, mistakenly believing Sue to be up to no good, intervenes to keep Sue from stopping Chris, and the circle of misguided actions and beliefs is complete. Heart-stopping in its presentation, the lead up to Chris yanking the rope that tips the bucket of blood down onto Carrie is as impressive a sequence in horror cinema as it is in De Palma's genre-crossing oeuvre. The tension ratcheted up throughout the slow-motion sequence finally gives way to full blown horror as De Palma invites the audience into the mind of his central character at the very moment her adolescent, human confusion turns to monstrous revenge. It is at this point that *Carrie* the movie and Carrie the character don't just toy with audience expectation and identification, they annihilate it.

THEY'RE ALL GONNA LAUGH AT YOU!

Where there is tension, there must be release, and the consequence of Chris' prank occurs entirely within Carrie's mind. With only the creaking sounds of the dangling rope heard, the movie pauses to allow the full horror of what we and the prom-goers have just witnessed, and Carrie has just experienced, to sink in. Given the previous shot of Chris licking her lips in sexualised anticipation, it is a metaphorical post-coital moment of respite before reality kicks in; except 'reality' and 'fantasy' for Carrie have now become so confused that her mind cannot differentiate between the two. In base terms, it is at this moment that Carrie goes mad. As 'reality' dawns on her, De Palma places the audience inside Carrie's tormented psyche as a kaleidoscope of images and repeated dialogue flood our collective eyes and ears. By drawing us in, De Palma also contradictorily begins to distance us from Carrie; the swirling images of the prom-goers all united in howling mirth are plainly figments of Carrie's imagination. That she repeatedly hears her mother's warning '*they're all gonna laugh at you*', Miss Collins' assurance '*trust me Carrie*' and Principal Morton's insensitive but well meaning '*we're all very sorry, Cassie*' informs us that the lines between guilt and innocence, between actual reaction and imagined reaction, have become irrevocably blurred in her mind. It is because we know that the majority of the assembled witnesses share in her horror that our identification with the beleaguered victim/hero/monster is thrown into confusion.

As Carrie is reborn, this time as a 'monster', De Palma splits the screen – she is figuratively divided in two, the screen literally, and the viewer thrown off one set focal point, one identifying hook on which to hang our collective hats. Carrie's revenge is pure spectacle; hose pipes move with serpentine stealth, doors slam shut as the doors to Carrie's mind are locked into furious anger and water and fire consume the prom-goers without mercy; the destruction of Sodom and Gomorrah as envisioned with tuxedos, high heels, pop music and mirror-balls. The death of Miss Collins – fittingly crushed by a falling piece of sports equipment (a basketball headboard) – a deviation from the novel in which Miss Desjardin survives, points to Carrie's inability or refusal to differentiate between 'good' and 'evil', 'right' and 'wrong' and 'guilt' and 'innocence'. Miss Collins' death is also symbolic; in killing her Carrie kills a version of herself that she may, one day, have become. Similarly symbolic are the deaths of Principal Morton and the English teacher, Mr. Fromm. Prideful but ineffectual, they both clamour for a microphone on the stage, desperate to take charge but utterly unable to stop the chaos around them. They are both electrocuted as water meets electricity to create fire; elemental forces adding another Biblical touch to proceedings. The panic stricken prom-goers become a faceless mass under Carrie's judgemental eye, with De Palma taunting us with her monstrosity. Mere moments after she has elicited our deepest sympathies, she is at her most repulsive.

De Palma turns Carrie's vengeance into a pointed comment on the nature of viewing, on cinema as being emotionally manipulative. David Thomson's entry on the director in the fourth edition of his *Biographical Dictionary of Film* (2003), states that '*he is the epitome of mindless style and excitement swamping taste or character*', going on to assert that '*he has contempt for his characters and his audience alike, and I suspect that he despises even his own immaculate skill*' (2003: 226). To my mind, De Palma's 'mindless style' is anything but, his visual excessiveness perfectly in sync with Carrie's monumental powers. The 'excitement' of the scene is contentious, as it turns the camera onto the audience, we watch the horror unfolding as entertainment; but it is a horror perpetrated by the one we have held closest to our hearts. Character is not swamped by style in *Carrie*, character *informs* the style – technical prowess is employed as it fits Carrie White, a girl with an extraordinary gift. De Palma doesn't hold his characters, the audience or his own skill in contempt; he employs his skill to create a dialogue between character, narrative, audience and film. He has no interest in presenting a straightforward revenge narrative, his interest lies in the surrounding factors that could push someone to the edge and beyond, our apparent pleasure in watching it unfold and in distorting conventions so as to question our voyeuristic desire for violent spectacle. If we are to view violence as entertainment, De Palma will make sure that our emotions are fully engaged. It is through the distancing techniques utilised – the divided screen, audio manipulation and the violent acts themselves – that the viewer is reminded of having invested time and emotion in the one carrying out those violent acts. Rather than Thomson's view that De Palma falls prey to '*narrow-minded movie mania*' and indulges in '*cold blooded prettification*' (ibid.), in *Carrie* De Palma is in intense conversation with his audience; beauty and horror, reality and fantasy and empathy and revulsion are as inextricably bound together in life as they are in onscreen entertainment. De Palma is ruthless, but, like Carrie, he displays an anguished ruthlessness. Far from being rigidly callous or cruel to his protagonists, De Palma is in love with his characters, as he is with cinema as an art form. It is not, however, a blind love; he accepts that 'good' people do monstrous things, and that 'bad' people sometimes deserve our deepest sympathies. The challenge for all of us is how we judge Carrie after she has reaped her revenge. The horror evoked in the prom night sequence is as clear a demonstration of this as Carrie's display of supernatural power is a clear physical manifestation of her inner torment.

THE CLIMAX

The Devil has come home.

The final sequence proper in *Carrie*, one that occupies ten minutes of screen-time, is a two hander between mother and daughter in which their bond is a conduit for the institutions of family and Church to be shredded as the consequences of a maniacal attitude to sex, death and religion culminate in attempted infanticide, successful matricide and self-destruction. The shifting power relations between mother and daughter are represented through dialogue and movement as images previously seen are mirrored, blood continues to be a symbolic presence and Donnagio's score resembles a dirge. A subliminal deconstruction of the state of the family and religion in contemporary America underpin a horrific clash between generations; a violent, corrupted vision of the bonds between adult mother and adolescent daughter. Hitchcockian in construction (through editing and sound), Biblical in meaning and tragic in effect, the climax literally collapses Carrie's world around her ears, a physical implosion to mirror her inner breakdown.

Returning home from the prom in a state of shock, the blood-drenched Carrie finds the house silent and illuminated by hundreds of candles. The household, already 'infused with a religious fever' is now to all intents and purposes transformed into the inside of a church, the family home rendered in reverential images and tones and exacerbated by Donnagio's score . Peeling off the prom dress, thereby shedding an embryonic skin, Carrie bathes herself, washing away the remnants and the memory of the prom. Returning to a pre-menstrual, pre-adult state – child-like in appearance and devoid of make-up – Carrie is effectively reborn again. By now her mother, viewed half in shadow, has clearly transcended mere fervour and entered into outright mania. Fully disconnected from even her own obtuse vision of the world, Margaret is now, in her mind, an avenging angel, a position occupied by Carrie during the prom. De Palma rejects King's version of the final confrontation between Carrie and her mother, in which daughter returns home with the express intention of ending her mother's life in favour of one in which Carrie is once again pushed into utilising her powers in response to a traumatic incident. De Palma employs his oft-used tactic of colour changes to signify that Margaret is now corrupted – her black clothes replaced by an all white gown, just as

Margaret's death pose is the mirror image of the statue of St Sebastian

Tony Montana's suits change from black to white in *Scarface* the more he is consumed by his own madness. In De Palma's world, white is often the colour of evil, of a poisoned soul, and here it solidifies Margaret's descent into dangerous instability.

Kneeling before her daughter, in apparent submission, she launches into a crazed soliloquy dominated by religious references to sin and the Devil, bemoaning her 'back-sliding' and admitting to enjoying the sex with her drunken husband that eventually led to Carrie's birth. Drawing her daughter, literally and metaphorically, down to her level to pray, she stabs Carrie in the back with a kitchen knife, sending her tumbling down (always down) the stairs. Heaven, Purgatory and Hell are once more metaphorically deployed, the upstairs of the house providing a Heavenly retreat for Carrie, a sanctity where her mother is angelically dressed in white. The ground floor of the house is the Purgatory in between the two polar opposite states, and mother and daughter are sucked down into Hell as the house collapses and sinks into the ground below.

Their positions now reversed, with Margaret looming over Carrie, ready to kill her – a priestess making an offering of a sacrificial lamb – Carrie sends a host of kitchen implements flying into her mother's body, pinioning her to an open door-frame. A gender reversed double of the statue of St Sebastian, Margaret moans in a discomforting mixture of pleasure and pain, a Grand Mort as a Petite Mort, the sexual abandon of an orgasm pointedly linked to the moment of death. The beatific expression Margaret's face assumes in death is evocative of that seen on the face of the *Beata Beatrix*, Dante Gabriel Rosetti's Pre-Raphaelite, symbol-heavy representation of spiritual transfiguration at the moment of death. That the 'release' Margaret felt during sex with her husband, feelings that triggered her over-riding guilt and shame, emotions physically embodied by her daughter, can only be appeased by a fatal return to those feelings drives home the links Margaret makes between sex, death and religion in her mind. Sexual penetration and bleeding from the orifices is recalled by the penetrating of Margaret's body by the kitchen utensils (ironic phallic implements, given their association with feminine home-making under patriarchy), her fresh orifices bleeding as if in mirrored sympathy with her daughter's menstrual bleeding, the catalyst for all that followed.

As Carrie first signified her horror with a scream in the shower room, she does so again as the consequences of the unleashing of her awesome power begin to sink in. This final rupture to her mind, a supernatural intrusion into her 'real' world, destabilises that world for the last time, as the White household collapses in on itself, the 'family' imploding under the weight of its own lies, emotional ties and fears. Hollywood's predilection for representations of dysfunctional families in horror movies during the seventies finds its bleakest outlet here. The Sawyer family in *The Texas Chain Saw Massacre*, for example, is painted as grotesque; wholly unsympathetic figures stripped of human qualities, and created to instill fear into audiences. Damien Thorn is the Anti-Christ in *The Omen*, a purely malevolent entity whose destruction of the family home is a microcosmic forerunner of his plans for all of humanity.

The White family is more recognisably human; Margaret may act like a monster and Carrie is capable of monstrous acts, but they are not monsters *per se*. The divisions between the human and the monstrous are not just blurred in *Carrie*, they are destroyed. As Paul states, '*if the human is the monstrous, as the collapsing Manicheanism of this film suggests, most monstrous of all is the bond between mother and child*' (1994: 368). Fear is instilled, but so is empathy – we fear them *because* we recognise them. The maniacally religious Margaret and the supernaturally gifted Carrie may be exaggerated and fantastical respectively, but the tortuous strains evident in their mutually dependent relationship are simply expressionistic visions of the self same struggles between dependence and independence that the majority of us experience with our own parents and/or children.

The familial landscape set out in *Carrie*, one dominated by absent fathers, frustrated housewives and adolescent daughters on the cusp of adulthood reflects the increase in broken homes in contemporary society and the fascination for examining every aspect of teenage life that has arisen since the 1950s. Where once American movies would have had dutiful daughters in stable homes presided over by paternal figureheads, by the time of *Carrie* the situation was markedly more pessimistic, even if it was more like the world as many experienced it. Mental abuse, rebellion, transference, oppression and eventually violent destruction act as a gloomy representation of the state of familial, hence social, cohesion in 1970s America. The generation gap, religious mania and familial breakdown had never been more brutally represented than at the moment Margaret White plunged the knife into the back of her daughter; adolescence betrayed by adulthood, a daughter rejected by the mother whose parental instincts are driven by fear, guilt and repression. Margaret's oppressive attitude towards Carrie begets a self-fulfilling prophecy – '*the Devil has come home*' – for her because she is partly responsible for her daughter's status as 'other', 'witch' and 'monster'. Youth, however, has the power in *Carrie*, and by the return of the repressed, the old order is overturned – but in overturning it, youth is itself condemned and destroyed. As a vision of society at the time, it is excoriating in its pessimism.

THE CODA

Carrie White Burns in Hell!

After everything De Palma put the viewer through in the preceding ninety minutes, one may be forgiven for thinking that *Carrie* would draw to an (un)natural, tragic conclusion as the White house collapsed in on the dying Carrie and her dead mother. Unfortunately for Sue Snell and the viewer, however, De Palma conceived of a post-narrative sequence that would shock, delight and infuriate. Shock because of its unexpectedness, delight because of the thrill of that unexpectedness and infuriate some as it defied narrative closure and further twisted audience identification issues, issues that had been played with since the volleyball match that initially welcomed unsuspecting audiences into Carrie's world.

Playing out as a literal nightmare reverse of the dreamy slow motion section of the shower room sequence, the coda performs much the same action; luring the viewer in before delivering a nasty surprise. This time clearly signposted as an actual fantasy scene, rather than the shower room's appearance/intimation of being one, by first showing Sue asleep in her bed before entering her subconscious, the sequence again demolishes expectations. Carrie White's bloodstained hand reaches up out of the grave to grip Sue's arm as she places the wreath on a makeshift cross, with 'For Sale' written on it and 'Carrie White burns in hell!' daubed over the top, planted into the vacant lot where the White home stood. Cars traveling backwards along the road, a shift from daylight to darkness (by the use of day-for-night photography), and the sudden switch from a lyrical to a staccato soundtrack jolt Sue, and the viewer, from the realms of the merely unusual to the blatantly horrific. The house of cards De Palma has reveled in knocking down time and again in the movie is once again rebuilt and sent tumbling. Are we to believe that Carrie White is the 'evil' force suggested by this sequence? Why have we suddenly assumed the viewpoint of Sue Snell? Does the introduction of an actual fantasy sequence nullify what has gone before it, where fantasy has carefully been integrated into reality? For Kim Newman it does: *it's the old hand-through-the-window shock tactic, but never has it been as devastatingly executed as it is here. It may well be the best cheap shot in the cinema, but it cancels out the film that precedes it*' (1988: 124). This endlessly imitated sequence, one that absolutely scared the living daylights out of me on first viewing and still thrills to this day, is as much about the experience of cinema as it is about Sue's parlous mental state following Carrie's revenge. Far from canceling out the film that precedes it, however, the sequence solidifies what we have witnessed and our allegiance shifts to Sue Snell with good reason.

In much the same way as Carrie's telekinetic powers rupture the screen and the soundtrack during the movie, so her hand reaching out of the grave grabs onto not only Sue's arm, but metaphorically onto the viewer's as well. The bloodied stain left on Sue's arm in the nightmare, and hence left on her memory in waking life, is one that also smears the memory of everyone who sees it. Paul drew the same conclusions in *Laughing Screaming*, stating that '*it was as if the movie continued to have some hold on us (much as Sue's mom held onto Sue), exerting a control that reached us even in the cold reality of the illuminated theatre*' (1994: 409). Even in death Carrie White is still there, shaming us with her 'shame', implicating us not only in her torment but also in her terrible vengeance – grabbing onto our thoughts with bloodied limb. The sequence doesn't define Carrie White as a witch or a monster, though she assumes this position in the sequence; rather it leaves a trace memory of her that lives on outside of the cinema, either of her character or of those real Carrie Whites, those 'others', female or male, we know or have known in our lives. Newman states that we have been 100 per cent with Carrie throughout the movie until this moment, whereas Clover posits that although the majority position is Carrie's, '*the camerawork repeatedly invites us to take the position of Carrie's sadistic tormentors (a familiar feature of De Palma's direction)*' (1992: 8). I believe that De Palma invites or tempts the viewer to occupy the mindset of all of the central, and some of the secondary, characters at one point or another. There is a fluidity of identification instilled in *Carrie*'s narrative, or at least in De Palma's version of it, that is intrinsic to the movie's ability to unsettle, confuse and linger in the memory. Ambiguity regarding identification plays a weighty role in how *Carrie* the movie wheedles its way into the viewer's subconscious, just as Carrie the character does into Sue's. De Palma's pessimism taints everyone involved onscreen and off, and it is through the shifting of viewpoints from one character to another that enables the rug to be pulled from under the feet of viewers who have occupied those multiple viewpoints. The movie reminds us of those things we would rather not be reminded of; memories secreted in the backs of our minds that return to haunt us just as Carrie returns to haunt Sue's subconscious.

Those onscreen may be individual entities, but those offscreen, by their voyeuristic, God-like ability to assume the position of Carrie, Sue, Margaret or Chris, become one – an all seeing eye that regards what is happening, understands why it is happening but can do absolutely nothing to stop it from happening. Through this manipulation of our expectations and identification, De Palma leaves the viewer as tormented as Carrie and questions whether they are as judgmental as her mother and as guilty as her tormentors. That is a horrifying position for the viewer to occupy, more damning and uncomfortable than the restricted view that Carrie White is a 'monster', or that the movie is inherently misogynistic. If one looks to *Carrie* for a clearly delineated, neatly packaged tale of 'good' vs 'evil' in which closure is reached by the restoring of the natural order, then disappointment will follow. The narrative and its presentation are therefore complimented by the inclusion of the coda sequence, not weakened. For Paul, '*Carrie's ending was the most direct assault yet on closure's dominance in Hollywood films'* (1994: 410), entirely fitting for a movie in which the misty eyed view of school days being the best time of our lives is mercilessly skewered. There is a reason why the beginnings of both the shower room and coda sequences have a soft-focus look about them: all the better for De Palma to slice through that image and give us one whose clarity is matched only by its horror. There is no bright spot at the end of *Carrie* to relieve that horror; rather, we are left with a sour taste in our mouths, one that De Palma thinks we collectively deserve. Robin Wood sums up the man and the movie in a way that cements *Carrie*'s position as one of cinema's bleakest horror movies and underlines how, rather than being misogynistic, *Carrie* is an all encompassing indictment of patriarchal authority:

> For Brian De Palma, the cultural situation is beyond any hope, social change is impossible, and all one has left is to enjoy the fascinating spectacle of corruption and disintegration as best one can. (1986: 129)

CONCLUSION

We're all very sorry, Cassie.

In Roger Ebert's review of the movie, the critic notes that '*Carrie is a true horror story. Not a manufactured one, made up of spare parts from old Vincent Price classics, but a real one, in which the horror grows out of the characters themselves*'.[6] It was De Palma's success in so resolutely grounding the horrors witnessed in human terms that aided *Carrie*'s transcendence from the usual limitations and conventions of the genre. Sad, moving, kinetic, symbolic, pessimistic, recognisable and fantastic, *Carrie* is fluid in meaning and representation, leaving the viewer as unable to gain a sure footing as the teenage telekinetic. It is a Greek tragedy with the Stars and Stripes draped around its sagging shoulders; the Old World in New World's colours. *Carrie* went postal before 'going postal' became a regularly renewed stain on the collective consciousness of American life. The titular teenager is now synonymous with high school loners, both onscreen and off, such was her torment and revenge, and such was Spacek's rendering of the character. If *Carrie* had passed unnoticed, as many of the subsequent thematic takes on it did, there would be no real evidence for its inclusion as a classic of horror cinema. Like Carrie White at the prom, though, the movie did not pass unnoticed; it made a significant mark, a bloodstain if you will, on the horror genre; both adapting to, differing from and permanently altering it.

It's '*showy brilliance*',[7] rather than being a distraction, is essential to the narrative's moments of explosive horror. Tonal shifts, from romanticism to reality and comedy to horror, reflect the constantly fluctuating moods of the adolescent lives at its heart; a time of discovery, experimentation, cruelty and hi-jinks. Lyricism and savagery go hand in hand in *Carrie*, it's a female *Lord of the Flies* even with figures of authority, the supposed sanctuary of the family home and the rigidity of a school schedule present; the law of the jungle within an urban environment. If '*Hell is a teenage girl*', as the opening line of the Diablo Cody penned teen-horror *Jennifer's Body* (2009, Kusama) attests, then Carrie White was its clearest representation to that point. Not just because of the monstrosity of Carrie's revenge, but because her mere existence, demeanour and status causes such ripples of consternation, emanating out from her mother, through her teachers, via her peers and back to the teenager herself. Jennifer (Megan Fox) and Dawn (Jess Weixler), the teen blessed/cursed with *vagina dentata* in *Teeth* (2007, Lichtenstein), are just two of Carrie White's children, their own horrific experiences – as victims, avenging angels and monsters – a constant reminder of *Carrie*'s teen-angst blueprint. Similarly, the menstrual theme present in *Ginger Snaps* (2000, Fawcett) and *Excision* (2012, Bates Jnr.) (both more graphic in terms of onscreen violence and more cutting in terms of dialogue than De Palma's movie) rely on the memory of *Carrie* as a stepping-stone to their confrontational depiction of the monthly cycle. The 'horror' of *Carrie* is that she is trapped; by birth, environment and reputation. There is no way out for her other than to self-destruct, to implode/explode under the incessant stares of those around her. Taunted, manipulated and constantly oppressed, Carrie White never really stands a chance. The over-riding sense of futility felt throughout the movie, knowing, even on first viewing, that something very bad lies in store for her, compels the viewer to keep watching. That is perhaps the cruelest trick played in *Carrie*, the one the director plays on his audience. He questions our desire to watch, like rubberneckers passing a crash, the humiliation, revenge and aftermath wrought on and by the central protagonist. The 'monster' that stalks our nightmares in this movie is one to be found on every street, in every classroom and in all of our collective and individual memories. In the era when '*horror comes home*', Brian De Palma led us up the garden path (literally and figuratively), into a gloomy household and into the tortured, doomed life of Carrie White.

FOOTNOTES

1.   A sea snail and marine gastropod mollusc family, the Cowry's shell has been legal tender and used in tribal religious ceremonies.
2.   *Senses of Cinema*, issue 3, 2000.
3.   *Refractory: A Journal of Entertainment Media*, 26 December, 2008.
4.   In 'Carrie: Ragtime—The Horror of Growing up Female' in *Jump Cut*, no:14, 1977, p.9-10.
5.   In his review of *Carrie* from 17 November, 1976, Richard Eder also draws parallels between De Palma and the Pre-Raphaelites.
6.   *Sun Times*, 1 January, 1976.
7.   Alan Brien, *The Sunday Times*, 16 January, 1977.

PART 4: LIFE AFTER DEATH: *CARRIE'S* LEGACY

The influence of Brian De Palma's *Carrie*, in terms of themes, structure and milieu, would be felt across not just the horror genre but also the comedy genre in the late 1970s and early '80s. *Carrie's* focus on adolescents, its 'final scream' sequence, pre-occupation with bodily emissions, victim/hero/monster central character, contemporary settings and pop culture references within a genre-straddling narrative would be referenced by and provide the inspiration, in one form or another, for a multitude of subsequent movies. As Magistrale notes: '*De Palma's* Carrie *initiates a cycle of teenage film comedies* – Animal House, Porky's, Fast Times at Ridgemont High – *that celebrate the physical gross-out, the adolescent body out of control*' (2003: 24-25). *Carrie's* other main contribution to the gross-out comedy movie was in terms of milieu and the character traits of its inhabitants. The high school, or other educational establishment, became a regularly used setting, with the Queen Bee, school jock, nerdy hangers-on, ineffectual adults, delinquent boys and sexually promiscuous (bordering on nymphomaniac) girls all becoming stock-in-trade characters. *Carrie* didn't create the character types or instigate the milieu, but it cemented them in the minds of film-makers and film audiences. Similarly, the movie's impact on the horror genre saw it begin

> ...a cycle of teenage horror flicks featuring the adolescent body under vicious assault, films such as *Halloween*, *Friday the 13th* and *A Nightmare on Elm Street*. *Carrie* presents itself as a unique blend of both teen genres, highlighting the disturbing links between adolescence as a time of silly misadventures and encroaching violence. (ibid: 25)

Carrie's distinction lay not in it being the first horror movie to centre on a group of young people '*under vicious assault*' in a contemporary setting (specifically an educational environment) – Bob Clark's 1974 proto-slasher *Black Christmas* was set in and around a sorority house – or in it being the first to use psychic/supernatural powers as a central narrative theme. What *Carrie* did was popularise its distinct elements within its singular narrative that film-makers, of horror, comedy or comedy-horror films, then used, consciously or unconsciously, as noticeable elements in their own films.

Carrie's central narrative hook – the use of telekinetic/psychokinetic powers – had been utilised as a major or minor plot device in a number of films and television shows prior to both King's novel and De Palma's movie. Stretching as far back as Lothar Mendes' 1936 film adaptation of HG Wells' 1898 short story, *The Man Who Could Work Miracles*, but largely from the late 1950s onwards, telekinesis/psychokinesis had cropped up on both small and big screens in the science fiction, horror and comedy genres. A cultural increase in interest in psychic phenomena during the '60s and '70s – the era in which self-proclaimed psychic Uri Geller was a regular on television shows around the world – had not gone unnoticed (and was perhaps aided) by writers, film-makers and producers. On television, episodes of *The Outer Limits*, *The Twilight Zone*, *My Favorite Martian*, *I Dream of Jeannie*, *Bewitched*, *Studio One*, the animated kids cartoon *Jonny Quest* and the British kids show *The Tomorrow People* all featured characters blessed/cursed with supernatural powers, sometimes used altruistically or mischievously and other times malevolently. TV movies and theatrical releases in which telekinesis and/or psychokinetic powers were displayed included *4D Man* (1959, Yeaworth Jnr.), the British entry *Fiend Without a Face* (1958, Crabtree), *The Power* (1968, Haskin – itself a remake of a *Studio One* episode) and *Psychic Killer* (1975, Danton), a low budget oddity released a year prior to *Carrie*. Literary sources again formed a thread through the emerging screen visions of telekinetic/psychokinetic powers, from Wells' *Miracles* via Amelia Reynolds Long's 1930 short story, *The Thought Monster* (the basis for *Fiend Without a Face*), to both versions of *The Power*, which were drawn from Frank M. Robinson's 1956 novel of the same name.

The precedents for reader/audience interest in psychic themed narratives are plain to see, but it was De Palma's *Carrie* that would become the lodestone for all future movies in which telekinesis/psychic abilities played a key role. The fact that *Carrie* remains superior in almost all respects to the vast majority of the movies directly influenced by it is more a testament to the strength of De Palma's vision of King's material than it is to any shortcomings, though there were many, in the films – be they horror, comedy or comedy-horror – that share thematic, stylistic and structural similarities. For an in-depth look at 'gross-out' horror, comedy and horror-comedies, Paul's *Laughing Screaming* (1994), which features an image from *Carrie* on the front cover and one from *National Lampoon's Animal House* (1978, Landis) on the back, is the book to which one should turn. Many of the other critics and academics that I have cited in this study – such as Robin Wood, Kim Newman, Pauline Kael and Carol J. Clover – have between them written in detail about the film (positively, ambivalently and negatively) and its impact on the horror genre as a whole. The 'final scream' coda sequence is now such an established part of horror genre film-making that it is more of a shock to not see it employed. Cine-literate audiences know there will likely be one final post-climax moment designed to make them jump and/or leave the door open for further entries in a franchise. The shock impact this scene had on unsuspecting audiences at the time has been replaced with knowing, even weary, expectation. The hand-out-of-the-grave sequence, once radical and itself inspired by the end shot of John Boorman's *Deliverance* (1972), has become a convention of the genre; there to be conformed to, parodied, consciously avoided or redefined. The victim-revenge narrative, not instigated but complicated by *Carrie*, has continued to appear regularly as a narrative set up in the horror and thriller genres. The character type of Carrie White herself – helpless/dangerous, attractive/repellent, heroic/monstrous – became a whetstone for a changing genre in which gender and audience identification issues were being redrawn for culturally, socially and politically changing climates.

Along with the TV movie adaptation of *Carrie*, *The Rage: Carrie 2* and the stage musical, the existence of a sub-genre of films directly influenced by the movie, that broadly fit into what Kim Newman calls the 'Psicopath' film, strengthens the position *Carrie* holds as a classic of horror cinema. Newman describes the sub-genre as revolving around '*seemingly ordinary individuals with hidden, awesome paranormal powers*' in a narrative framework that sees '*the Psicopath humiliated, abused and pushed beyond endurance, whereupon immense mental powers are unleashed in an orgy of mass destruction*' (Newman, 1988: 46). The sub-genre, which Newman extends to include Satanic possession movies and which has *The Omen* and *Carrie* as its touchstone reference points, may have been relatively small in number and short in life span, but in watching any or all of the entries into it where psychic powers are at play one cannot avoid drawing comparisons with De Palma's movie. Of course, *Carrie* was and is not alone in spawning a host of imitations, sequels, remakes and derivations; but along with the likes of *Night of the Living Dead*, *Jaws*, *Alien* (1979, Scott) and other genre changing/defining movies it is precisely because of its revolutionary/evolutionary nature that it is so often recalled and used as a blueprint for those other movies.

Leaving aside Satanic possession movies, the three films that most clearly resemble *Carrie* in terms of themes, narrative structure and milieu, are the made for TV movies *The Spell* (1977, Philips) and *The Initiation of Sarah* (1978, Day), and the theatrical release *Jennifer*. These films all centre on a young, socially awkward female with a troubled home life who is blessed/cursed with psychic powers. The powers are unleashed in acts of revenge against their (predominantly female) peers and/or adults in positions of authority, and are (largely) set within a high school, a sorority house and an exclusive private school respectively. Released within two years of *Carrie*, they all suffer in comparison first and foremost because of their overtly derivative nature. Although it may appear to be unfair to compare made for television movies with a theatrical release, given that TV movies are generally regarded as the lesser of the two forms, the deficiencies apparent in them reflect the depth of intelligence seen in De Palma's movie. Rita (Susan Myers) in *The Spell* may be bullied for being overweight, Sarah (Kay Lenz) may target the girls from a rival sorority house and Jennifer (Lisa Pelikan) may display her powers through the ability to control snakes (handily available in her father's pet shop), but the viewer is ostensibly watching a version of Carrie White. Additionally, a combination of any or all other detrimental elements – lower budgets, weaker scripts, unmemorable casts and performances and less rigorously controlled direction – offer little to mitigate the coattail riding nature of the films.

1978 saw the peak of the 'Psicopath' film, with a number of other variations on *Carrie*, in which themes, narrative structures and milieus diverted but drew inspiration from De Palma's movie, gaining theatrical releases. De Palma's own follow up to *Carrie* was another adaptation of a novel revolving around psychic powers and the psychological trauma wrought on those blessed/cursed with them; John Farris' *The Fury*, first published in 1976 and adapted for the screen by the author himself. Along with *The Fury*, the British-French co-production, *The Medusa Touch*, directed by Jack Gold and adapted from Peter Van Greenaway's 1973 novel, and Richard Franklin's 1978 Ozploitation shocker, *Patrick*, all sought to capitalise on the unexpected box office and critical success of *Carrie*. These films have less directly in common with *Carrie* in terms of milieu than *The Spell*, *The Initiation of Sarah* and *Jennifer*, but in their narrative structure and themes they have many similarities. The central protagonist, or protagonists in the case of *The Fury*, possesses telekinetic powers which are unleashed in increasingly destructive fashion throughout their individual narratives, each culminating with one last shocking display of that power. The diversions taken from *Carrie*'s narrative, while at least making for a more rewarding viewing experience than the direct rip-offs, highlight why the movie is the Urtext of its sub-genre.

The Fury revolves around the manipulation of two psychic twenty-somethings, Gillian (Amy Irving) and Robin (Andrew Stevens), by a shadowy Government agency, within another genre-crossing piece by De Palma, this time a horror-thriller. Off the back of *Carrie*, producer Frank Yablans handed De Palma his biggest budget to date – $5.5 million – with the hope that the director would exceed his previous movie, in both the artistic and financial stakes. *The Fury* certainly goes far beyond *Carrie* in its blend of kinetic action and graphic violence, and its narrative is on a grander scale than the hermetically sealed world inhabited by Bates High School's teens. But what *The Fury* lacked, just as many of the other movies inspired by *Carrie* did, was a central figure, or figures, as rounded, prominent and recognisable as Carrie White.

Telling the tale of secret service agent Peter Sandza's (Kirk Douglas) search for his son Robin, kidnapped by Sandza's superior, Childress (John Cassavetes), to be trained as a psychic-weapon and used for political blackmail, *The Fury* sacrifices the emotional heart and universal themes inherent in *Carrie* in favour of more straightforward action thrills. De Palma's fascination for split personalities and doubles continues – this time in the figures of Robin and Gillian, who is drawn into Peter's search, the 'good' father/'bad' father figures of Peter and Childress and in the nurturing, scientific environment of The Paragon Institute in opposition to the rigidly controlled, militaristic, exploitative surroundings where Robin is incarcerated. Described as 'psychic twins', Gillian and Robin, who both struggle with their untutored powers and are generically assigned as 'good' and 'evil', feminine and masculine figures, are clear equivalents of Danielle and Dominique in *Sisters*, and more pertinently, Carrie White. As with *The Spell* and *The Initiation of Sarah*, this literal division of personalities, while conforming to De Palma's thematic interests, waters down the rich complexity of tensions and emotions seen in the single figure of Carrie White.

The director continued to deploy and refine the auteurist techniques with which he is associated – 360 degree camera movements, split-dioptre shots, symbolic colour schemes, slow motion – and the film contained another Hitchcockian/Herrmannesque score, this time composed by John Williams, performed by the London Symphony Orchestra and, according to Pauline Kael '*as elegant and delicately varied a score as any horror film has ever had*'.[1] Despite containing sequences as thrillingly realised as any in the director's career – a fog bound car chase, Gillian's escape from The Paragon Institute and Robin's destruction of a Ferris Wheel being on a par with the split-screen bomb scene in *Phantom of the Paradise*, the prom night massacre in *Carrie* or the split-level hotel climax of *Raising Cain* – *The Fury* was neither a critical or box office success. Mixed reviews and box office takings of $11 million do not constitute a failure, but it does point back to *Carrie*'s boundary crossing appeal – critically and commercially. Where De Palma invested time and energy in the characters in *Carrie*, and rigidly controlled the moments of tension and release, in *The Fury* he relegates these elements in favour of an overt desire to explore style, technique and effects. In *Carrie*, De Palma achieved a balance between style and substance missing from *The Fury*, and from many of his other films. The hermetic world of *Carrie* – small, tightly focused, familiar – struck a lasting, resonant chord that *The Fury* – grand, sprawling, exclusive – couldn't emulate.

The foremost departure from *Carrie* in *The Medusa Touch* and *Patrick* is in gender terms. Both central protagonists, Richard Burton's John Morlar in *The Medusa Touch* and Robert Thompson's titular character in Franklin's movie are more recognisably malevolent. Embittered, physically damaged and bent on causing havoc, they are 'monstrous' masculine figures. The cross-genre, cross-gender appeal of *Carrie* and Carrie White is replaced by a conservative gender and genre narrative in both movies and both central figures. *The Medusa Touch*, a supernatural whodunnit, centres on the destruction caused by misanthropic novelist Morlar before and after being left comatose as a result of attempted murder; and in *Patrick*, another coma patient wreaks jealous havoc from his hospital bed on the life of his nurse, Kathy (Susan Penhaligon). Seen through the eyes of seconded French detective Brunel (Lino Ventura) and nurse Kathy in Gold and Franklin's movies respectively, the narratives shift the emotional centre, and hence the audience's focus of identification, away from the 'monster' that *Carrie* so firmly embeds into the heart of its tale. Necessary as this shift is to both narratives – with their monstrous figures both lying comatose – they become more conservative as a consequence; less emotionally uncomfortable for the audience and more traditional in appearance.

Morlar and Patrick evoke little more than fear in the other characters and revulsion in audiences. This leaves them more aligned with Hannibal Lecter in *The Silence of the Lambs* (1991, Demme) and Henry in *Henry: Portrait of a Serial Killer* (1986, McNaughton) than with the Creature in *Frankenstein* or Seth Brundle in *The Fly* (1986, Cronenberg), to which the figure of Carrie White bears relation. *The Medusa Touch* and *Patrick* are devoid of the underlying emotional resonance, pop culture zeitgeist and genre-altering milieu that De Palma brought to the screen. It is the eschewing of a complex dialogue between film-maker/writer and audience in relation to the 'monster' figure in their works – and the use of a masculine figure to embody that 'monster' – that makes *The Medusa Touch* and *Patrick* ultimately less rewarding and interesting – critically and academically – than De Palma's movie. The masculine figures at the centre of these movies are simply not critically stimulating enough in comparison to the changing representations of women in the horror genre at the time. While *Patrick* was nominated for three Australian Film Industry awards, and both films subsequently, and deservedly, gained cult status, *The Medusa Touch* came in for a critical battering on its release. The film was slammed, by amongst others Gene Siskel and Roger Ebert, who dubbed it *'the worst film of 1978'* for its resemblance to *Carrie* and Burton's perceived overacting.[2]

After the initial outburst of psychic/telekinetic movies, the sub-genre continued but the direct influence of *Carrie* became less readily apparent. Narratives, narrative structures and environments began to differ – though all movies retained at least some aspect of De Palma's movie – with the telekinesis/psychokinesis theme being the most overt, and conscious, link back to it. Largely low budget theatrical or straight to video releases, these films attempted to tap into the appeal of *Carrie* with their own tales of psychic horrors, but added little of critical or academic value to the panoply of issues addressed in De Palma's film. An unofficial sequel to *Patrick* emerged from Italy in the form of Mario Landi's gaudy exploitation flick, *Patrick Vive Ancora* (*Patrick Still Lives*, 1980), along with the intriguing, Pino Donnagio scored, stalker/slasher cum psychic horror of *Tourist Trap* (1979, Schmoeller), the corpse re-animating psychic siblings of *Kiss Daddy Goodbye* (1981, Regan) the teen-centric *One Dark Night* (1983, McLoughlin) and the American set, British production, *The Sender* (1982, Christian). David Cronenberg's *Scanners* (1981) strayed from the telekinesis theme to centre on telepathic and psychokinetic abilities, though it noticeably, like *The Fury et al*, featured opposing 'good' and 'evil' figures struggling, mentally, with their abilities, the power it bestows and its uses rather than *Carrie*'s premise of a singular embodying emotional focal point.

In 1984, the fifth adaptation of a Stephen King novel within a year, *Firestarter*, again recalled *Carrie* as well as highlighting the author's own recurring use of characters blessed/cursed with psychic powers and interest in exploring issues surrounding innocence and its loss. Bearing structural and thematic similarities to *Carrie*, *Firestarter* failed to match the critical interest in and box office takings of De Palma's movie as well as suffering in comparison to David Cronenberg's contemporaneous take on King's *The Dead Zone* (1983), another psychic-themed narrative. *Firestarter* centres on a young female – Charlie, played by Drew Barrymore – who has a pyrokinetic gift/curse which she uses to devastating effect in the film's climax. Though used not to take revenge on classmates but to escape the clutches of a secret Government agency bent on exploiting her powers *a la The Fury*, *Firestarter* is a clear thematic and structural sibling to King's debut novel and De Palma's idiosyncratic take on it. As with the central characters in many of the related films, the figure of Charlie conjures up the image of Carrie White, and King's own redeployment of a narrative featuring a young female – this time a child rather than an adolescent – struggling with overwhelming powers and surrounded by malevolent figures, is indicative of the lasting power of that image and that scenario. The sub-genre never gained the traction of the slasher, the zombie or the torture porn movie, though the films in its category do indicate *Carrie*'s lasting impact.

Carrie's timeless themes and enduring popularity led to a subsequent life away from the big screen in other media. Lawrence D. Cohen conceived *Carrie: The Musical*, at the time a much publicised production that would eventually be classified as one of Broadway's most expensive flops. Cohen began work on the production as early as 1981, with composer Michael Gore and polymath Dean Pitchford – Academy Award winners in the Best Original Song category for 'Fame' from Alan Parker's 1980 film of the same name – recruited to provide the production's music and lyrics. Announced as an on-Broadway show in 1986, with funding secured in 1987, *Carrie: The Musical*'s production costs ran to $8 million, a huge figure for the time. Produced by Friedrich Kurz and, perhaps incongruously, the Royal Shakespeare Company, the musical ran for four weeks in Stratford-upon-Avon in February of 1988 before transferring to the Virginia Theater, now the August Wilson Theater, in New York.

The initial UK run saw mixed reviews, songs excised and rewritten and veteran cabaret performer Barbara Cook, in her role as Margaret White, coming close to a fatal accident when an elaborate set piece went awry. The New York production fared little better, with yet more rewrites and some particularly scathing reviews – more lethal in the stage business than they are in the film business – leading to the musical being closed just three days after its official opening on 12 May 1988. Despite the show flopping on a grand scale, debutant Linzi Hateley as Carrie and Betty Buckley as Margaret White – who replaced Barbara Cook – were singled out for praise for their performances. Where *Carrie* the film saw impressive box office figures, spawned a raft of critical and academic analyses of it and catapulted King, De Palma and Travolta on to bigger, if not necessarily better, things, *Carrie: The Musical*'s lasting legacy was to inspire the title of theatre critic Ken Mandelbaum's 1992 book *Not Since Carrie: Forty Years of Broadway Musical Flops*.

Even this version of King and De Palma's material has, though, like Carrie White herself, refused to die. An unlicensed production of Cohen's show was performed at Stagedoor Manor – a performing arts summer camp in Loch Sheldrake, New York – in 1999, followed by another two unlicensed performances at Emerson College in Boston, Massachusetts. Further amateur performances of the show fittingly took place in high schools in Denmark and Scotland, with the Danish Gammel Hellerup Gymnasium Cast recording the show for release, in Danish, on CD. The show was again revived early in 2012, in an off-Broadway production by MCC Theater at the Lucille Lortel Theater in Greenwich Village, New York. Running for a month between 1 March and 8 April 2012, this more successful production, featuring revisions and new songs – overseen by Cohen, Gore and Pitchford – was nominated for several awards and plans for the first official cast recording of the production were announced by Ghostlight Records.

Additional stage variations on *Carrie* – drawn from the novel and the film – have appeared regularly, its cross-genre and cross-generational qualities being revisited for well over thirty years. Playwright Erik Jackson, with Stephen King's blessing, wrote a more comedic, camp and non-musical take on the material. The two hour and twenty minute show ran for a month at Performance Space 122 on 150 1st Street New York to sell out crowds in December of 2006. The spoofs *Scarrie! The Musical* and *Carrie White: The Musical* – a remake of Cohen's show – and the New Orleans-based comedy troupe Running With Scissors' *Carrie's Facts of Life* have all lovingly bastardised novel and film. These low-budget, underground productions prove an important point about the narrative, its themes and De Palma's visualisation of it: *Carrie* straddles a difficult line between provoking serious study while appealing to a pop culture audience. The youth-centric narrative, clearly defined character types and operatic levels of Gothic and gross-out horror have inspired camp, musical and comedic re-interpretations and parodies at the same time that its nihilistic, symbolic obliteration of family, state and religion led to critical deconstructions that have themselves become seminal texts applied to the study of the horror genre.

In keeping with Hollywood's penchant for sequels, remakes and reboots, Katt Shea's *The Rage: Carrie 2*, initially titled *Carrie 2: Say You're Sorry*, saw the light of day in 1999. Another troubled production, with original director Robert Mandel quitting over oft-quoted 'creative differences', *The Rage: Carrie 2* closely followed the narrative trajectory of De Palma's movie. Drawing its plot from a real life high school sex scandal,[3] *The Rage: Carrie 2* sees outsider Rachel's (Emily Bergl) latent telekinetic abilities first triggered by a stressful incident (the suicide of a friend) and finally unleashed to murderous effect after a public humiliation (the airing of a sex tape in which she features), before the obligatory Final Scream sequence. On the plus side, Clover's Final Girl in Shea's movie is a Final Boy, with Jesse (Jason London), the boy to whom Rachel loses her virginity in the sex tape, the sole surviving, and psychologically scarred witness to the climactic revenge massacre. Bergl's central character is the movie's major weakness; she is more of an outsider in the fashion and gossip stakes than a genuinely awkward, out-of-time figure like Carrie White.

The revelation that Rachel is Carrie's half-sister – they share the same absent father – ties the two narratives together, and Rachel's humiliation does, to its credit, highlight an issue – the exposed sex tape – that is a regular occurrence in the modern world. Produced by Paul Monash, Shea's sequel intercuts scenes from De Palma's movie and features the now adult Sue Snell as a student counselor. But devoid of the turbulent social, political and cultural context that *Carrie* emerged from and into, Shea's movie is ultimately undemanding, lightweight fare. Its '90s milieu, throbbing rock soundtrack and use of CGI effects render it as another derivative, unsuccessful and forgettable exercise in contemporary horror genre film-making. The *Carrie* format is applied so rigorously that once again the viewer is simply drawn back to De Palma's movie, not in ways that enhance *The Rage: Carrie 2*, but to its detriment. De Palma's blunt critique of religious oppression, complex representation of female sexuality and savage, literal and metaphoric, destruction of the high school environment failed to be followed up or superseded in Shea's sequel. A narrative that in theory was rich in promise – touching on institutionalisation, absentee fathers, desensitised sexual promiscuity, peer group pressures in contemporary society – is never fully explored in the script, its visualisation or the representation of its character types.

A more structurally faithful take on King's source material came in the shape of David Carson's made for television *Carrie* in 2002. Retaining the post-massacre flashback structure of King's novel – though The White Commission is replaced by a police investigation – Carson's *Carrie* also includes Margaret White's original death, the raining stones sequences and represents the widespread destruction of the town. Angela Bettis, who took the lead role in the similarly themed *May* (2002, McKee), made for a convincing victim and monster but lacked Spacek's ability to inspire the lust and emotional attachment in viewers and characters alike that was so integral to De Palma's vision. Poorly rendered CGI effects and a truly woeful original ending, possibly tacked on with the slim chance of a follow on television series in mind, in which Sue Snell (Kandyse McClure) helps Carrie to escape from the town in disguise, leave Carson's version of *Carrie* as a clumsy, ad-hoc mixture of King's novel, De Palma's vision of it and original material that only strips the narrative of its power. Patricia Clarkson gives a more studied, downbeat performance as Margaret White while the representation of Sue Snell is a major flaw. Unlikeable, defensive and duplicitous from the off – required though it may be to the plot, as she is under investigation regarding the absence of Carrie or her corpse – Snell is not the 'good' girl to Emile de Ravin's 'bad' girl Chris. Another integral part of De Palma's vision – the dual oppositional character types – is recalled by its absence in Carson's version.

In all of the derivations, remakes, sequels, reworkings and parodies, the crucial element missing is Brian De Palma. It took a hungry, single-minded director with an idiosyncratic, auteurist visual style to fully realise King's source material. De Palma achieved this by paring back that material to its bare bones and embellishing what remained with his own individualist stylistic and narrative touches. De Palma's *Carrie* has been evoked, overtly or subconsciously, since the day of its release, in films as diverse as *Revenge of* the Nerds (1984, Kanew), *Welcome to the Dollhouse* (1995, Solondz) and *Chronicle* (2012, Trank). One need only watch the documentary features on the 25th anniversary DVD release to see the genuine affection felt for the movie by those who made it and those who acted in it. For Amy Irving, '*to be in a horror movie with such eroticism, beauty and grace is a unique thing*',[4] while William Katt succinctly summed it up by stating that '*it changed the thinking about horror movies*'.[5] Pauline Kael, so often De Palma's foremost advocate, was at her insightful best when she posited that '*no one else has ever caught the thrill that teenagers get from a dirty joke and sustained it for an entire picture*'.[6] *Carrie* has beauty, horror and toilet humour as experienced by a lonely adolescent and envisioned through the eyes of a sometimes cruel, sometimes sympathetic but always provocative auteur. Playful, poignant, horrific and melodramatic, it is the archetypal teenage horror movie about the turbulent transition from innocence to experience, the power of female sexuality and the cycle of life and, ultimately, death.

FOOTNOTES

1. The New Yorker, 20 March, 1978.
2. In an episode of Ebert Presents At The Movies.
3. Involving 'The Spur Posse' in California in 1993; a group of high school boys using a points system to rate their sexual conquests who later faced charges, eventually dropped, of statutory rape.
4. From the 'Acting Carrie' documentary extra feature on the 25th anniversary DVD release.
5. Ibid.
6. The New Yorker, 22 November, 1976.

BIBLIOGRAPHY

Arnold, G. review of *Carrie*, Tri-City Herald, 5 November, 1976.

Ashbrook, J. (2000) *The Pocket Essential: Brian De Palma*, Harpenden: Pocket Essentials.

Bouzereau, L. (1988) *The De Palma Cut*, New York: Dembner Books.

Christie, I. review of *Carrie*, The Daily Express, 14 January, 1977.

Clover, C.J. (1992) *Men, Women and Chainsaws: Gender in the Modern Horror Film*, London: British Film Institute.

Collings, R. (1986) *The Films of Stephen King*, San Bernardino: Borgo Press.

Crane J.L. 'Come-on-a-my House: The Inescapable Legacy of Wes Craven's *The Last House on the Left*', in Mendik, X. (ed.) (2002), *Necronomicon Presents: Shocking Cinema of the Seventies*, London: Noir Publishing.

Creed, B. (1993) *The Monstrous Feminine: Film, Feminism, Psychoanalysis*, London: Routledge.

Ebert, R. review of *Carrie*, Sun Times, 1 January, 1976.

Eder, R. 'After the Prom, the Horror', The New York Times, 17 November, 1976.

Ewing, D. & Myers, D. 'King of the Road', American Film, June, 1986.

Greenspun, R. 'Carrie, and Sally and Leatherface Among the Film Buffs', Film Comment - Film Society of Lincoln Center, Vol. 13, iss. 1, January, 1977.

Grant, B.K. (1996) *The Dread of Difference: Gender and the Horror Film*, Austin: University of Texas Press.

Greven, D. (2008) *Medusa in the Mirror: The Split World of Brian De Palma's Carrie*, Refractory: A Journal of Entertainment Media - http://refractory.unimelb.edu.au/2008/12/26/medusa-in-the-mirror-the-split-world-of-brian-de-palma%E2%80%99s-carrie-%E2%80%93-david-greven/

Humphries, R. (2002) *The American Horror Film: An Introduction*, Edinburgh: Edinburgh University Press.

Kael, P. 'The Curse', The New Yorker, 22 November, 1976.

Kael, P. review of *The Fury*, The New Yorker, 20 March 20, 1978.

Kakmi, D. (2000) *Myth and Magic in De Palma's Carrie*, Senses of Cinema, http://sensesofcinema.com/2000/cteq/carrie/

Kent Bathrick, S. *Carrie: Ragtime – The Horror of Growing up Female*. Jump Cut, no:14, 1977, p9-10.

King, S. (1974) *Carrie*, London: Hodder and Stoughton.

King, S. (2000) *On Writing: A Memoir of the Craft*, London: Hodder and Stoughton.

Knapp, L.F. (2003) *Brian De Palma: Interviews*, Jackson: University Press of Mississippi.

Kristeva, J. (1982) *Powers of Horror: An Essay on Abjection*, New York: Columbia University Press.

Mendik, X. (ed.) (2002), *Necronomicon Presents: Shocking Cinema of the Seventies*, London: Noir Publishing.

MacKinnon, M. (1990) *Misogyny in the Movies: The De Palma Question*, London and Toronto: Associated University Presses.

Magistrale, T. (2003) *Hollywood's Stephen King*, New York: Palgrave Macmillan.

Magistrale, T. (1988) *Landscape of Fear: Stephen King's American Gothic*, Ohio: Bowling Green State University Popular Press.

Magistrale, T. (2008) *The Films of Stephen King: From Carrie to Secret Window*, New York: Palgrave Macmillan.

Mandelbaum, K. (1992) *Not Since Carrie: Forty Years of Broadway Musical Flops*, New York: St Martin's Griffin.

Nepoti, R. (1982) *Il Castoro Cinema: Brian De Palma*, Florence: La Nuova Italia.

Newman, K. (1988) *Nightmare Movies: A Critical Guide to Contemporary Horror Movies*, New York: Harmony Books.

Olsen, M. 'Flesh and Blood', Sight and Sound, October 2001, vol 11, issue 10.

Paul, W. (1994) *Laughing Screaming: Modern Hollywood Horror & Comedy*, New York: Columbia University Press.

Peretz, E. (2008) *Becoming Visionary: Brian De Palma's Cinematic Education of the Senses*, Stanford: Stanford University Press.

Salamon, J. (1991) *The Devil's Candy: The Bonfire of the Vanities Goes to Hollywood*, Boston: Houghton Mifflin Company.

Sobchack, V. (1978) 'Bringing It All Back Home: Family Economy and Generic Exchange', in Waller, G.A. (ed.), *American Horrors: Essays on the Modern Horror Film*, Urbana: University of Illinois Press

Stuart, A. (1976) 'Phantoms and Fantasies', an interview with Brian De Palma, Films and Filming, vol.23, no.3, issue 267.

Thomson, D. (2002) *The New Biographical Dictionary of Film*, 4th edition, London: Little, Brown.

Wood, R. (1986) *Hollywood From Vietnam to Reagan*, New York: Columbia University Press.

Wright, E. 'The Greatest Films of All Time', Sight & Sound, September 2012, vol 22, issue 9.

Zinoman, J. (2012) *Shock Value: How a Few Eccentric Outsiders Gave Us Nightmares, Conquered Hollywood, and Invented Modern Horror*, London: Duckworth Overlook.

DEVIL'S ADVOCATES

"Auteur Publishing's new Devil's Advocates critiques on individual titles offer bracingly fresh perspectives from passionate writers. The series will perfectly complement the BFI archive volumes." Christopher Fowler, Independent on Sunday

LET THE RIGHT ONE IN — ANNE BILLSON

"Anne Billson offers an accessible, lively but thoughtful take on the '80s-set Swedish vampire belter... a fun, stimulating exploration of a modern masterpiece." Empire

WITCHFINDER GENERAL — IAN COOPER

"I enjoyed it very much; it sets out all the various influences, both before and after the film, and indeed the essence of the film itself, very well indeed." Jonathan Rigby, author of English Gothic

SAW — BENJAMIN POOLE

"This is a great addition to a series of books that are starting to become compulsory for horror fans. It will also help you to appreciate just what an original and amazing experience the original SAW truly was." The Dark Side

THE TEXAS CHAIN SAW MASSACRE — JAMES ROSE

"[James Rose] find[s] new and unusual perspectives with which to address [the] censor-baiting material. Unsurprisingly, the effect... is to send the reader back to the films... watch the films, read these Devil's Advocate analyses of them." Crime Time

Printed and bound by CPI Group (UK) Ltd, Croydon, CR0 4YY

13/04/2025

14656610-0001